RIDING HIGH

By the same author

SOLDIER ON

The author jumping Teddy at Nice in 1939 when he won the 'individual' during the Nations Cup.

RIDING HIGH

*The Complete Guide To
Show Jumping*

Colonel Sir Mike Ansell

A. S. Barnes and Company
SOUTH BRUNSWICK AND NEW YORK

© MCMLXXIV by Colonel Sir Michael Ansell

Library of Congress Catalogue Card Number 77-74116

A. S. Barnes and Co., Inc.
Cranbury, New Jersey 08512

FIRST AMERICAN EDITION PUBLISHED 1978

ISBN 0-498-02100-9

Printed in the United States of America

Contents

Acknowledgements

I wish sincerely to thank Mr Denis Goacher for correcting my indifferent English, as he did when I wrote *Soldier On*.

I should also like to thank Miss Judith Robinson for her drawings which had to be done from my explanations, and of course I thank my old friend, M. Jean Bridel for the excellent photographs and for arranging with M. Tissot to have them reproduced from *L'Année Hippique*. My grateful thanks are also due to Mr Leslie Lane for his admirable photographs, and I wish to thank Mr Bruce Crunden of Rose, Crunden Associated Ltd, for arranging for the various diagrams to be drawn.

My list of those to whom I owe thanks would be endless, but once again my gratitude to Miss Sally Doman for much retyping, and to Mr Ronald Attwood for reading to me.

Finally my grateful thanks to Captain Webber, to Mr Alan Ball and all those of the British Show Jumping Association who provided such excellent data on measurements and distances.

I only hope that this book will help young riders who wish to train their horses, and also those who build the courses and organize the horse shows that provide such great enjoyment for everyone interested in equestrian sports.

Illustrations

*Except where otherwise indicated, photographs are by
courtesy of* L'Année Hippique

[xiii]

CHAPTER I

A Curtain Raiser: Oflag IX A/H

In the late summer months of 1941, three British officers, all of whom had show jumped for Great Britain before the war, found themselves together in a P.O.W. camp: Oflag IX A/H, Spannenburg, Deutschland. The three were Lt. Colonel 'Bede' Cameron, RHA, Major 'Nat' Kindersley, RHA, and Lt. Colonel 'Mike' Ansell.

Tedium was a spectre we all hated the sight of, and most of us there were absolutely determined not to waste the long hours of what we'll call our enforced leisure. So courses abounded, carefully organized by officers drawn from a seemingly unlimited number of peace-time occupations. You could learn about agriculture, accountancy, law. You could learn how to make a tweed suit out of a blanket, or a rubber stamp from the heels of your shoes. You could even learn how to pick locks and to fashion keys that would guarantee you an 'open sesame' anywhere!

All these courses were well attended and one of the most popular, I think, was that on Equitation. We had the advantage of 'Bede' Cameron having been the chief instructor at Weedon, and both Nat Kindersley and I had been instructors over long periods. Another much involved was Major Guy Hanmer of the 19th Hussars—incidentally a very talented artist; I remember his doing wonders with coloured crayons on old German newspapers.

The equitation course, after we'd covered the intricacies of riding and horsemastership, was expanded to take in the more individual sports: hunting, polo, and fatefully, as it turned out, show jumping. The three original musketeers had all jumped for Great Britain as I've said, but obviously we'd also competed in the various national shows.

[1]

Now these took place under the rules of the B.S.J.A., whereas the international shows were governed by the Fédération Equestre Internationale. Show jumping under the F.E.I. rules was unquestionably more attractive for horse, rider *and* the spectator; it must be remembered that enthusiasm for this sport on the continent in pre-war days could be compared with, say, fox hunting in England. The story of how these two sets of rules were ultimately reconciled is rather long and involved; I've told something of it in my autobiography, *Soldier On*, and needn't deal with that here.

During one of my lectures at the camp these obsolete rules were carefully explained, while Guy Hanmer provided endless coloured illustrations of the courses, fences and general layout: they hung around the walls on a surfeit of German newspapers. (It seems rather appropriate, looking back, although we little guessed that in years to come we would often flatten the Germans handsomely at the sport in which they were then more or less supreme). In these lectures I tried to work out what the future of show jumping in Great Britain might be, and how we could make it more *fun* for everybody. At the conclusion of each talk I gave a couple of 'commentaries'—I still have the texts, stamped with the official GEPRÜFT of the censor. They ran more or less as follows:

First I set the scene for my fellow officers: a one- or two-day agricultural show, pre-war. We imagined that we were fortunate enough to be sitting next to an elderly gentleman who understood all that was going on, and consequently could explain the open jumping competition to us. As the last class of show hunters left the arena, two other somewhat younger gentlemen—obviously the judges—stepped out importantly into the centre, each with a large white scoring card. One in a grey bowler was undoubtedly the local Master of Foxhounds; the other, not so smart, possibly the farmer on whose land the show was being held . . . These two judges sit on their shooting sticks, quietly surveying the arena, as our elderly friend in the stand explains the course. The first fence is made of hurdles with well packed gorse, the second a red brick wall—but that's difficult to see from where we're sitting, for the wings are so large as to make a clear view impossible. The third is a triple bar. The horse will then come down our side and these jumps we can see more easily: the first of this line is a box of hurdles, again packed with gorse, the distance looks not more than twelve feet or so, and of course the horse must jump in *and* out. A white gate follows and the third is a stile, the latter looking very flimsy. The rider then swings down the centre to number 7, a water jump, which seems to be giving trouble as some of the men are busy patting the clay edge with their spades. Two or three chaps stand at each fence, and they're already busy replacing slats on top of the rails and gate, as fast as they blow off in the wind! Well, that's the course, all ready.

Whatever's happening now? . . . A mass of riders, some in cloth caps, some in bowlers, even some in military uniform are entering the ring. Oh yes, of course, their mounts must have an opportunity to study these fences. This takes quite a time for each fence must be carefully inspected by the horse—who not infrequently takes a bite of the gorse, or pushes a pole of the triple down with his nose . . .

But now we really are ready to start and after a further short delay the first rider, wearing a large number, sets off. Over the gorse hurdles, no trouble there. Difficult to see at that triple but certainly a slat went, half a fault. Now down our side—yes, he's jumped the in-and-out with ease. Now the gate, another slat's gone, but surely no fault of the horse! He jumped miles over it. Yes, we were quite right, it was only the wind. My goodness, though, the stile has gone in all directions. The judges are arguing like mad, and while the men are frantically trying to put the thing together again they're asked whether the horse hit it with forelegs, belly or hind legs? Eventually they give the rider the benefit of the doubt: hind legs, two faults. Next, the water. The rider's having a little trouble as he circles near the collecting ring and undoes the quick release on the martingale—now he's off! Gosh, what a splash. Well, not so bad as it might have been, the judges have decided it was only three legs in the water, one fault for each foot. Three faults, then, and a total of five and a half.

There now seems to be a bit of delay. No one wants to come in. Just as well, for the men are busy with their spades at the water that has shown signs of escaping.

Ah, but now we're well away; this lady on a short tailed cob is jumping superbly. One, two, three, 'hup'. Now steady, back to a trot, as she approaches the gate. Oh, what bad luck, it's blown down. However, quickly corrected, and again one, two, three, and 'hup'. No faults yet, and she's approaching the water: a few circles while the martingale is undone, and away she goes, the first to clear.

And so the competition progresses. 4 faults if knocked down with forelegs, 2 with hind legs, a half for a slat down. Should the horse refuse within the wings, one fault, 3 for a second refusal, and third, out. But my friend explains that provided the horse doesn't go into the wings—no fault. Many ticklish problems for the judges to decide: How many feet in the water? Was the obstacle hit with forelegs, belly, or the hind legs? As for those wretched slats, was it the horse, the wind, or even the horse's tail?

Nevertheless, the competition slowly advances and the stands slowly empty. Finally there are nine horses equal without fault. The judges hurry around raising each fence. Exciting, for there are only four prizes. We're ready. Why no riders? Ah yes, five are coming in now to talk to the judges (of course they're not mounted). We gather that the competitors have decided all nine should divide the prize money; they don't wish to jump again. As we leave the stand we see the gallant nine entering for their rosettes. The secretary looks forlorn since he only has four rosettes. Well, that won't matter, they can toss for it!

The scene in our small room in the P.O.W. camp looked very changed as Guy Hanmer, Nat Kindersley and Bede Cameron pinned up an entirely different set of pictures of the course we envisaged for the future. It was based on those then in existence on the continent. Fences gay with flowers, shrubs and coloured poles. There would, we explained, be no long delays, as competitors walked quickly on their own two feet round the ring. The three judges would be sitting in the stand, as the first horse entered as drawn: Some fourteen or fifteen fences to be jumped, well built affairs with wings small and in line with the fence, so that all could see and judge. If a fence fell, 4 faults: if the horse refused or circled, 3 faults—and if a second time, 6 faults and then for the third, elimination. The competition would speed on, and if at the close there were four remaining without fault, all would jump again. If still equal, the fastest time was the winner.

The strange thing is that we in Oflag IX/AH never imagined that these and similar changes would come so rapidly in Great Britain.

In 1952 I published a small book on the building of obstacles and courses. Colonel Haccius of Switzerland, possibly one of the greatest of all course builders, was kind enough to write in his foreword:

'As he (Mike Ansell) rightly says the responsibility of building the course is too often left to anyone. It is essential that the person responsible for this important task, must have the necessary practical experience gained from riding across country and in the show ring. Without this experience the builder will not be in a position to judge the standard of the riders and horses, and so set a course fair in height and layout, taking into consideration the conditions of the ground. In addition the competitors should be satisfied and the interest of the spectators held. Further, a good imagination is required in order to create frequently what is new and to break away from certain monotony when building courses.

'Good obstacles, well presented, imposing and solid in appearance, make good jumpers, others make horses careless and slack . . .

'The test for horse and rider will first be the nature of the obstacle, the height and the width. Regarding the distances between the fences, I think there are easy distances, difficult distances, and false distances. The builder must decide upon the object of the test he intends to set, the rider must then adapt his riding in order to succeed in this test. Do not, above all, think there is only one good distance as this would be a mistake. When setting the course consider the conditions and *guard against the abuse of the importance of time, which if abused, does not improve either the rider or the horse.* The use of ground lines must be carefully considered, and not used to remove the natural characteristics of an obstacle.'

The whole world acknowledges that, in the twenty years and more since those wise words were written, Great Britain's progress in the art of show jumping has been quite staggering.

CHAPTER II

Choosing Your Horse

Nowadays show jumping has come so much to the fore that, unless you are very rich, you're unlikely to be able to afford a horse which has proved its ability. In the past, jumpers seemed to come in all shapes and sizes, from the finest to most indifferent breeding, but the standard is rising all the time and now your only hope is to find a good young horse at a reasonable price, and train it yourself. The question is, what do we look for? Answer, a horse whose conformation will make it easy to train.

The horse of prehistory was an animal with short legs, about the size of a fox. It could survive, not requiring much speed, because it lived on the plains. During the course of evolution it became necessary for it to gallop to evade its pursuers, but it never acquired the physique and ability to jump great heights—as in the case of the cat family.

Now our constant search is for a horse which *is* capable of tackling an ever greater height and spread, and each year the fences must be jumped with greater speed and accuracy. Our only consolation can be that great stamina is not required, for show jumping courses are short, rarely more than 800 metres. All types *may* succeed, but it is only sense when purchasing a young or 'green' horse to search for a perfect build—as with any athlete, swimmer, footballer or whatever, the conformation must matter. The better the conformation, the easier it will be to train. And training is everything.

Looking over your would-be purchase, he should have an attractive head, well set, with a large kind eye. The head carried not too high, a neck not too long but at the same time supple. Prominent withers, a good sloping shoulder, long forearm and a short cannon bone, average

[6]

slope of pasterns, a good foot. The great Mr Jorrocks said 'no foot no 'oss', therefore beware of flat soles but look for nice flat heels, with a good frog and bars. Lifting up the foot you should find it saucer shaped and concave. I cannot stress enough how desperately important the foot is, for your show jumper will often have a good deal of hard going, and there is a world shortage of top blacksmiths.

In India, when not working on metalled roads, we never shod our horses for much of the year, except possibly with 'tips', and consequently the horses' feet were broad, the frogs well developed.

Never forget that, when landing over a large fence the foot, and the frog in particular, takes much of the concussion. A severe test, if you remember that a horse weighing ten or twelve hundredweight is dropping five feet or more at about twenty miles an hour.

Next, have a good look at your 'possible' with a saddle on. It should sit in the right place, i.e. not too low down. Behind the saddle we'll hope to see good strong loins with plenty of length—after all the loins matter so much in jumping. A good length from hips to hock then, and strong hocks are of equal importance.

In motion I like to see a light free movement somewhat like a ballet dancer, with a short rather than long stride in the canter. He must have a good mouth, and I'll hope to find he has a short lip. Height is obviously a consideration for although in recent years we've seen wonderful small horses of not more than 15 hh, and great horses of over 17, I personally would favour 16 or 16.2 hh.

Temperament—well that's of the utmost importance, good nature the essential for both horse and rider. I've already recommended looking for a kind eye, hoping that the human eye would be just as kind.

Some years ago I was sitting with Mr Andrew Massarella, Mr Len Carter and Mr Bob Hanson. We discussed various types of show jumping horses and you would be hard put to find three more knowledgeable persons in this game. 'An eye for a horse', the saying goes, but how do we come to possess that secret? Few can pick a good horse even if fit and well turned out, fewer still when in the 'rough'. This wisdom and judgement will only be found among those who've had unlimited experience, some of it alas bought dearly.

These three certainly had the knowledge though I don't know what it cost them to acquire it. Len Carter bought and rode show jumpers for some fifty years, Andrew Massarella had literally thousands of all types of horse through his hands, and when I was Brigade Major of the 5th Cavalry Brigade, Bob Hanson owned some nine hundred horses each year. So I was fortunate to be able to listen to these three philosophers of the horse world. It's often suggested that the type has changed in recent years, but that's true only in the sense that a would-be purchaser of means cannot now *afford* to buy anything but the best, the most suitable.

We've already agreed that some exceptional jumpers differ considerably in origin and even conformation: Stroller a pony, Nizefela not superbly bred, Prince Hal a thoroughbred, Tosca (with all politeness) in a different class altogether, Fox hunter a three-quarter thoroughbred. Nevertheless, as we are going to spend so much time on the training of a horse it is surely better to start with the most suitable and orthodox material.

The transcription which follows may be repetitious in parts but advice such as this is truly worth pondering. Without it, I certainly wouldn't be in a hurry to buy a potential show jumper.

Len Carter: 'I go a lot by what I see when I first see him, if I don't like him at first looks I don't try to buy him. He must have a nice head, eyes, and ears which really move and work. Head set on his neck nicely and not upside down. A jumper must have strong loins and never be hollow backed. His legs and feet are most important, good open feet, flat knees and joints not round ones.'

Bob Hanson agreed, and emphasized that he did like a horse with a good head, plenty of room between the eyes, as he will then have a bit of common sense. If you don't like the head you don't want the horse. *Andrew Massarella* added: 'If he hasn't got the gift to jump he won't make a top class jumper, but you are certainly more likely to find that gift in a well made horse.'

Bob Hanson: 'What I say, Andrew, is that if you have the conformation right then you're home. The well made horse will be the easier to train.'

Len Carter again: 'I do like to see a horse, when he walks, walk clean. I don't want to see him 'daisy cut'. I like to see them on the short stride, if they're long striding they find it more difficult to get right on the approach. A show jumper should have a good knee action, it helps him if he can bend his knee a bit.'

Discussing colour all three experts agreed they didn't like blacks or mulish-coloured horses. They usually had a bad temperament. Simi-

i. 'I do like to see a horse walk clean.'

larly, all preferred browns, or bays with black points, though Andrew Massarella didn't mind chestnuts if they had a touch of white—he thought it was rather like an attractive lady with a touch of rouge or lipstick. Unfortunately these chestnuts were sometimes a bit 'hot'.

Bob Hanson further emphasized the importance of the foot and everyone sympathized with the plight of the present day jumper, the combination of hard going and lack of good blacksmiths making for very severe strain. A good blacksmith always paid particular attention to the frog, which takes so much of the impact when landing.

These three were then shown photographs of famous past jumpers: I'll only quote their remarks about two of them.

COMBINED TRAINING

This brown gelding with a star, 15.3 hh, foaled 1901, bought in Ireland, had his first success with Major-General Geoffrey Brooke at Olympia in 1912. He served throughout the First War. After the war his wins were numerous and in 1921 he won the King's Cup. He, like Broncho, was a member of the first British Team to win the Prince of Wales' Cup in 1921.

[9]

Andrew: 'Now this is a fine horse. This is the type of horse I like. Look—a good big sheath—a sign of strength. Well, gentlemen, never forget this. Whether it be a cart-horse, a van horse or a jumper, that horse has one thing you should always look for. If you buy a horse with a good sheath, he will always have some power to him.

'We have one now, Bob, that isn't bigger than 15.3 hh; he's as strong as a lion. You could yoke him to this hotel and he'd not stop pulling till he had it down. It's a real sign of power. I remember in the old days the first thing a farmer used to look at was the horse's sheath. "Has he got a good sheath under him, Tom?" "Yes—you go and buy him—he's a topper".'

Bob: 'A really nice horse—a beautiful shoulder, sloping well back. He's cocky, well put together, with a nice short back. This horse would carry fifteen or sixteen stone. Look at his sweet little head. That's the nicest head of all these.'

ii. Combined Training—brown gelding 15.3 h.h.

Andrew: 'There again, look where his tail is put on—right high up, that is the place.'

Len: 'You'd certainly call this horse perfectly coupled, and good round the girth.'

Andrew: (studying the pictures of Broncho and Combined Training), 'Well, gentlemen, if you wanted my candid opinion here definitely, if a man went on and bought either of these horses, he wouldn't be far wrong. We all agree that these are the horses we look for. Broncho has a bit more quality perhaps but you, Bob, would take home Combined Training first. If only we could find them, we would buy them and they'd jump.'

So finally, Broncho, which everyone agreed is the type of horse you long to discover, buy, and then start training.

iii. Broncho—*bay gelding 16.3 h.h*

BRONCHO

A bay gelding with a star, standing 16.3 hh, known throughout the world with his great rider, Lt. Colonel Malise Graham. After the First War, when over twenty years old, he came into his best. He helped Britain to win the Prince of Wales' Cup for the first time at Olympia in 1921. From then on he had numerous successes, particularly at the International Horse Show.

Andrew: 'Now this, to my mind, is the ideal horse. This is the type of horse that is wanted today. That's the class of animal we all look for.'

Bob: 'I agree. Look at his head—beautiful. I think perhaps he might have a little more front to him. He's got plenty of room for his heart. His depth, his back and his loins are really good and strong. He looks to have legs and feet like iron. His knees and fetlocks are really perfect.'

Andrew: 'That's the horse I would buy for a show horse, a hunter or a jumper, or anything.'

Len: 'Let alone jumping, you'd bid for that horse without seeing him move. You'd know that you had a horse you'd sell as a show horse if he didn't have that gift to jump.'

Andrew: 'Well, gentlemen, I look for this type of horse everywhere, and any one of us would feel he'd done a good day's job if he found him.'

These two horses are what we all look for. Handsome is as handsome does, but today—more than ever before in jumping—the handsomer he is the easier he will be to train. And win.

CHAPTER III

Early Days

We'll assume that, having taken some expert advice, we've now bought a four-year old, well nigh perfect in conformation for jumping. But although he's been bred with this purpose in mind, has been backed and ridden, he hasn't in fact yet been jumped. How do we set about training? Much of what I'll write here I learned over long years from Colonels Paul Rodzianko, J. H. Dudgeon and V. D. S. Williams, and from experience gained at Saumur, the French Cavalry School, on prolonged visits during the years 1931, '32 and '33.

To gain my horse's confidence I take him for walks on a lunging rein; at the same time he'll learn to obey my voice. He must learn to obey unerringly the commands of 'halt', 'walk on', 'trot' and 'canter'. He'll be bridled with a large ringed snaffle, the reins knotted, and with a drop nose-band fitted three finger breadths above the nostril—with the back strap in the chin groove. I use that drop nose-band to prevent the horse putting his tongue over the bit, which is a difficult habit to correct; it will also stop him crossing his jaw. I place a cavesson over his bridle; the nose-band of the cavesson may go under or over the cheek pieces of the bridle but must not interfere with the snaffle bit. I then attach my lunging rein to the centre ring. This lunging rein should be about 23 ft long, made of web. When on the near side I lead with my right hand, holding the coiled up lunge rein in my left, together with the long whip. Conversely, from time to time I'll lead the horse on the off side, thus leading with my left hand and carrying lunge rein and whip in the right. That whip is seldom if ever used for punishment; it merely does the job my legs would do were I mounted. That is to say, leading my horse I walk level with his forelegs and,

[13]

iv. 'I take my horse for walks on the lunging rein.'

when necessary, keep him pushed up slightly ahead of me with the whip.

Should we come across any little grips by the side of the road, or even small tree trunks, I push him gently over them and so he begins to learn to jump.

Once he is used to being led and is obedient to my voice, he's ready to be taught lunging. This has great advantages but it must be correctly done. We need a flat piece of ground out of doors or, better still, an indoor school.

Still carrying a saddle and bridle, my horse will be fitted with a lunge rein as for leading. For the first lesson or two we may need a second person who can lead him from outside the circle. I make him start from the halt. Standing in the centre, with my horse on the left, he is lunged with the rein in my left hand—the spare rein and whip held in my right.

[14]

I don't stand still all the time but keep moving for I must ensure that the horse is always 'between' my hands, the lunge rein, my legs and the long whip. So I contrive to stay at right angles to his hindquarters, keeping him pushed forward with my long whip.

Most lunging is done at the walk or trot. From the halt I give the command 'walk on', gently pushing him onwards with the whip, then 'trot', back to the walk, and 'halt'. Should I wish to steady him I quietly jerk the lunge rein with my hand making a very clear signal; similarly, when bringing him to the halt I make a definite signal by jerking the lunging rein. Halted, I call my horse to me saying 'come here' and at the same time walk back a few steps, drawing the whip along the ground and drawing him to me on the rein. When he reaches me he's rewarded with a pat and a bit of sugar or carrot; then I change the rein and he will do exactly the same on a right handed circle—'walk', 'trot', 'walk', 'halt', and 'come here'. Another reward, and change the rein once more.

As soon as my horse has learned complete obedience and will come

v. 'I contrive to stay at right angles to his hindquarters, keeping him pushed forward with my long whip.'

[15]

to me when I draw back the whip, indoors he can be lunged without a rein. The horse must then respond to my voice alone, but should I wish to steady him I simply give a jerk with my hand—the horse will be watching that hand as though I had the rein in it.

We'll assume now that this horse is entirely obedient to my voice: much of the work has been done at the trot but he may even have been lunged at the canter. Although he's learned to negotiate small ditches or logs, the next stage is to train him to jump in earnest.

In a sense the horse was never built to jump—compared with a dog or a cat for example. The cat's muscles and tendons were evolved specifically for jumping. Horses have eighteen pairs of ribs while dogs have thirteen and cats only eleven; consequently the horse doesn't have sufficient space between rib cage and pelvis to be a natural jumper. I know it's often said that such and such a horse *is* a natural jumper but that's probably only true because he's been bred to jump. Furthermore, as with any athlete, runner or hurdler he must be taught what has been discovered to be the correct style.

Approaching a fence, your horse lowers his head and instinctively judges the take-off. At the moment of take-off it's essential that his head should be lowered, forelegs driven into the ground, for it takes

vi. 'At the moment of take off it is essential that his head should be lowered.'

[16]

vii. 'In flight the head should still be lowered, enabling the horse to arch his back.'

viii. 'When his forefeet hit the ground his head is raised.'

weight off his hindquarters and thus gives them maximum freedom and impetus to drive the horse over the fence. In flight the head should still be lowered, enabling the horse to arch his back, completing a perfect parabola or bascule. Throughout the jump your horse uses head and neck to maintain his balance—much as a tight-rope walker uses a long pole—and when his fore-feet hit the ground, the head is raised.

So over the next few weeks I must concentrate on getting my horse to use head and neck properly and to arch his back while jumping. Of course there have been horses which have jumped successfully with a flat back, but they've been few, and who knows how much greater they might have been had they learnt the orthodox way.

CHAPTER IV

Training on the Flat

'o enable this horse of mine to produce his best, I establish a definite rogramme. Although I am already lunging him I must also gradually et him used to weight on his back. Therefore, in order, I will first ide him, then lunge him, and follow up with a peaceful hack in the ountry—taking a light lunge rein in my pocket.

Only in comparatively recent years have the majority of horsemen cognized the immense importance of training on the flat before aching a horse to jump mounted, and the virtue of continuing that aining throughout his competitive career as a show jumper. The eat French horseman, La Guerinière, who lived over two hundred ears ago, explains 'the aim of training the horse is to make him supple d obedient by systematic work'; and surely, to succeed in jumping, e horse must be both supple and obedient. La Guerinière adds, 'he en becomes pleasant in his movements and comfortable for his rider'.

This training on the flat is essential for the jumper because it velops him physically and mentally, and, more important, prevents due strain to sinews and muscles before they're ready—thus avoid- g the risk of their being over exerted or even broken down. Only e simplest exercises should be asked for at the start: strain will show ickly if the horse's intelligence or physical strength are overtaxed this point. The alternation of gradual training on the flat will also eak the monotony of asking the horse to jump too continually. These mple movements described below can often be done when out for a ck. Your horse will become mentally calm and happy and learn stant obedience.

His first lesson is mounting and dismounting. A horse must be taught

ix. 'Standing with the weight evenly distributed on all four legs.'

to stand quite still when being mounted. The rider should just put his
foot in the stirrup and pause, ensuring that the horse stands absolutely
still. Next he must put some weight on the stirrup: should your horse
move, the foot must be taken out and the exercise repeated until he
finally stands still; the leg can then be thrown over the saddle. This
standing still during mounting must be thoroughly confirmed before
moving off and the same applies when dismounting. Stationary, the
horse must stand with his weight evenly distributed on all four legs.

[20]

THE HALT: This is of the first importance because many movements, such as a turn on the forehand and transitions direct from halt into the trot or canter, cannot be performed unless the halt is good. Throughout his training the horse should always be made to stand squarely, with the hind legs well under him; he will then get into the habit.

THE WALK: As will now be clear, the horse must not be allowed to move off unless he is standing quite still and correctly, and must only do so when he gets the order. Moving off he must remain on the bit and not throw his head up: if he does so he must be halted at once and the movement repeated until the transition is made correctly. Now he should be given his head and walk on with a long swinging stride.

x. 'Keeping the horse on the bit or up to it is extremely important.'

[21]

Before starting any lesson it's a good thing to make a horse walk out on a long loose rein. During the early days of training one must not on any account, do 'collected' work at the walk: this will shorten his stride and inevitably cause him to get behind the bit.

A horse is said to be on the bit when he accepts it with his head in the correct position and his hind legs well under him. Much of this training is to ensure the horse makes the best possible use of his muscles. If the hind legs are under him properly, the back will become rounded, the haunches lowered in consequence. If he raises his head above the natural position he will hollow the back, sending his legs out behind him.

THE TROT: Keeping the horse on the bit, or up to the bit, is extremely important, and the rider must see that his horse remains on it during the transition from walk to trot. Again, he must not throw up his head: if he does, bring him back to the walk and repeat it, correctly. To move from the walk into the trot on a loose rein, the rider takes up his reins and squeezes with his legs; if the horse won't go readily into the trot give a gentle tap with your whip, behind the leg, or use the voice as when lunging.

As training advances, voice and whip should not be required, if your procedure has been correct. Our horse should now be pushed on at a good, light, lively trot, but no faster than he can manage or he'll begin shortening his stride and 'running'. If you train him well, as the horse's hocks get more under him, the stride will increase its length.

When the horse will go round on a large circle at a good, level pace, and you still feel the bit lightly on the reins, changes of direction and serpentines may be practised. In all such changes great care must be taken to maintain the same tempo and to keep him well on the bit.

THE CANTER: This can be attempted first from the trot on the circle. Your outside leg should be well drawn back, the horse urged into the canter by a firm pressure of both legs and a strong drive from the seat—your weight placed slightly on the inside. Should the horse not strike off on the required leg, bring him back to the trot and immediately try again. If he's been lunged thoroughly you will have little difficulty in obtaining a true canter on either leg.

Perhaps I ought to say here that too much attention needn't be paid to the head's position during early lessons but, once your horse understands what is required of him, you must be particularly careful to flex

xi. A good canter.

xii. 'Do not allow him to come off the bit by raising his head.'

him in the direction of his leading leg—and not to allow him to come
off the bit by raising his head.

To repeat: the correct aids for the canter, near foreleg leading, are
to sit down in the saddle, drawing the right leg back and pressing your
horse forward with the seat and both legs. Later the right leg may be
less drawn back. When the off foreleg is to lead, the aids must of
course be reversed.

On no account try for a collected canter during early stages: let it be
free and unconstrained with the horse 'carrying himself' and going
well forward. Pay strict attention to your transition back to the trot:
no propping, or concussion. The horse should go easily into the trot
without any apparent reduction of pace. You should concentrate on
making plenty of transitions from halt to walk, to trot, to canter and
back again. Then gradually reduce trotting until the horse will go
straight from walk to canter, and finally from halt to canter and back
to halt. Bear in mind always the importance of keeping your horse on
the bit and *straight* i.e. that the hind legs follow in the track of the
forelegs.

When the true canter is well established on both reins, the counter
canter, that is cantering to the left with the off foreleg leading and
vice versa, may be practised. Start by making a small loop from the
wall and back to the wall, gradually increasing the depth of your loop
until it comes well out into the centre of the school. When you can
achieve this without the horse changing his legs, without losing his
balance or increasing pace, you are ready to try changing the rein at
the canter, holding the counter-canter round the short end of the
school, and then change rein back again to the true canter. Through
out, your horse's head must remain bent in the direction of the leading
leg.

The counter-canter is an excellent balancing and suppling exercise
—very important for obtaining true changes of leg whenever required

THE TURN ON THE FOREHAND: this is a stationary movement, so
to speak, in which your horse revolves his quarters around the fore
hand. His inside foreleg (the one on the side to which the horse is
turning) is the pivot. So, turning to the right, the right foreleg is the
pivot and remains in place, while the horse carries his quarters to the
left, right hind leg over and in front of the left hind leg. The horse
must remain on the bit and absolutely not slide forward; he will be
slightly flexed to the right but the neck shouldn't be bent. As the

ider's right leg pushes the horse's quarter to the left, his left leg sup-
orts the movement to prevent the quarters from swinging too far.
urn completed, your horse moves forward without pausing.

HE SHOULDER-IN: this is the first exercise to practise in your work
n two tracks. You can start as soon as the horse answers to indications
rom hand and leg and will go freely forward at all paces, with a light
eeling on the bit. To obtain it, on your right rein for instance, take a
tronger feeling of that rein and bring the horse's forehand just off the
rack, hind feet remaining on the track. The horse is bent round the
ider's right leg, which in turn remains at the girth driving his horse
orward on two tracks. Left leg, applied behind the girth, prevents
indquarters escaping to the left and keeps up the impulsion. After
ie first few lessons it is better performed at the trot, for at that pace
ou can maintain impulsion more easily—and great care must be
aken not to lose this. The exercise should be terminated by perform-
ig a circle or turning across the school.

HE HALF-PASS AND THE TURN ON THE HAUNCHES: the differ-
nce between shoulder-in and half-pass is that, whereas in the former
our horse is bent away from his movement's direction, in the half-
ass he must always be bent towards the direction in which he's going.
   To perform a half-pass diagonally across the school, as soon as the
orse enters the long side he should be brought to the position of
noulder-in. Arrived at the diagonal marker, without altering the
osition of the horse's forehand you must make him move diagonally
cross the school on two tracks (to the corresponding marker on the
her side) by a stronger use of your outside leg.
   Another method is to ride a half-circle away from the wall, main-
in the bend and return on two tracks, at half-pass.
   For all practical purposes there are only these two lateral move-
ents: shoulder-in and half-pass. Both can be executed on a straight
ne or a circle, and you will devise many exercises for moving from
ie position to the other.
   The *turn on the haunches* is of course the converse of the *turn on the
orehand*: by this latter you've gained control of the haunches and
iould now have little difficulty holding them in place while he pivots
ie forehand round them. On no account allow the horse to take a
ep back—that would mean that he was not in front of the leg, and
eeping behind the bit. Outside foreleg must pass over and in front

[25]

of the inside one and, turn completed, your horse must continue smoothly forwards without pause.

THE REIN-BACK: Don't attempt this until your horse is completely and confidently between the rider's hand and leg. The horse must be pressed forward by the rider's legs into a fixed hand, when, finding no outlet for the impulsion produced, he will step back and should move forward as soon as the hand is relaxed. That backward movement must be absolutely straight and the steps, as pairs of diagonals should be of equal length. On no account allow the horse to run back out of hand, or drag his hind feet along the ground: fore and hind feet must be clearly picked up, to equal height, in two-time. The head may be slightly lowered but never raised. Above all, your horse must *never* be pulled back by the reins.

I've given these movements in great detail, because each year it becomes more apparent that in order to succeed a horse must be very thoroughly trained.

And so, having followed this system our young horse will show complete confidence in his trainer, who will continue to think carefully about what he intends to do each day. Monotony has to be avoided, which means regularly changing the routine. Always start, though, with ten or fifteen minutes of the movements described above, then go for a quiet hack to allow your horse to relax: take a light lunging rein with you if possible and from time to time dismount and go through those exercises—making sure that the horse answers meticulously to your words of command.

CHAPTER V

Lunging, and then Mounted

The time has now come for your mount to start jumping regularly and this should be done first on the lunge. Start with a pole or small log on the ground: he will jump these with ease, but you should always keep in line with the horse's hind-quarters, ready to push him on with the whip.

After a few days replace the pole or log with parallel poles, about 2 ft (.6 m) high with a spread of 3 ft (.9 m) – 4 ft (1.2 m). This will ensure that the horse looks with lowered head during his approach, and arches his back when jumping. That achieved, you may now start him jumping, still on a lunge, over individual fences, as in a course.

There should be six or eight, not more than 3 ft (.9 m) high and each with a spread, possibly a tree trunk, or a ditch and rail or parallel bars, but none of these must be large. In order to carry the lunge rein over the fence, a post with a thin rail should be on both sides as wings.

Lunge the horse on a circle before each fence, and when the trainer feels the horse is 'right' he should be pushed on over the fence. If he seems about to refuse at the last moment, the trainer should pretend nothing has happened but keep the horse going on the lunge until certain that he's ready—then push him over the fence. Immediately on landing, your horse must continue on the lunge and be gradually brought back to a walk, then the halt, and finally to the trainer and his well-earned reward, a piece of sugar. The trainer will start again at once, going from fence to fence, always keeping the horse on the move.

Now that he's supple and well balanced your time has come to jump

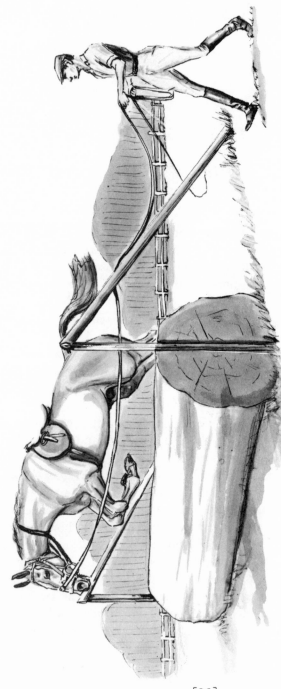

xiii. 'In order to carry the lunge rein over the fence, a post with a thin rail should be on both sides as wings.'

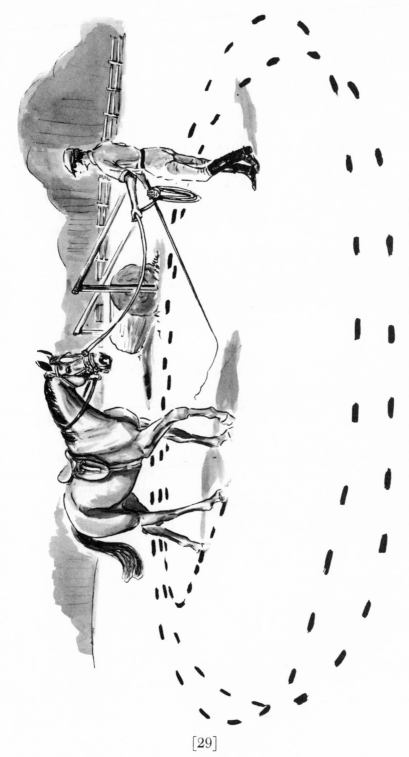

xiv. 'and gradually be brought back to a walk and then the halt.'

him mounted. Again I stick to a programme of daily work. Whether indoors or out, I first work him on the flat for ten minutes or so at the walk, trot and canter, and thoroughly loosen him up.

In the school or field we'll have seven or eight fences placed. Inevitably I use 'trestles' or cavalletti, about 2 ft 6 in (.8 m) high and 8 ft (2.4 m) wide on the approach. They're easy to move and when you want additional height one can be placed on top of two others. The trestles are placed as parallel rails: the spread starting perhaps at 3 ft (.9 m) and gradually increased to 6 ft (1.8 m). By using these, I make sure that my horse always uses his head and neck and jumps in a correct parabola or bascule.

We'll assume that he's loosened up and it's now time for his first jump mounted. I always have a breast-plate or strap round his neck to catch hold of, for when he jumps I'm determined to let him use his head, in no way interfering, yet maintaining contact with his mouth.

From the trot I jump one of the fences, circle around and tackle another; I jump these completely at random; on the approach I hold the neck strap or breast-plate, thus giving his head complete freedom, and so leaving it to him to put himself right. Whenever I feel his approach to be wrong, just as on the lunge I'll swing out on a circle and turn to another fence: in that way, I hope, he'll believe he was never intended to jump the other one.

For the first few days I'll probably jump him, mounted, over these trestles a dozen times or so; as time goes on I shall expect him to do thirty or forty jumps, possibly more. Circling, turning in sharply, still holding the neck strap, he'll gradually be confirming his style, with head down at the approach, correcting his stride, and then jumping in a perfect parabola or bascule. The jumping completed, we go off for a short relaxed ride—and it's always possible, if we come across a tree trunk or some suitable jump, I will dismount and take out the lunging rein, attach it to the snaffle and lunge him over it. So the days go by and we maintain this cycle: working on the flat, possibly some lunging, jumping over trestles or cavalletti, then a peaceful ride. To ensure your horse always makes an effort, at this stage jump out of a trot and never a canter.

My theme is obedience, suppleness, balance and complete trust between horse and rider. When I was at Saumur we used to be taken once a week to a 'sand track': it covered about half a mile (.8 km) and ran in a cross country circle, up and down hill with some very steep slopes. We were expected to trot or canter around and around this

xv. 'I will jump him, mounted, over these trestles.'

xvi. 'a length of old gas piping in front of the fence—if hit it'll make a good deal of noise but will not harm the horse.'

rack, always maintaining light contact to oblige our horses to balance hemselves, the rider sitting perfectly still. (On my return to Aldershot I used to make this a 'must' for the training of young horses or recruit riders.)

The horse is now ready to be introduced to larger fences, not more han 4 ft (1.2 m) or so: at these or greater heights your horse simply nust come 'right'. Normally he should take off approximately a height and a half before the obstacle. At a 4 ft fence it will be in a zone of between 4 ft to 6 ft from the base. Your horse must always be encouraged, so when first he tackles larger obstacles they should have a good ground line and be simply constructed, such as a hog's back.

Colonel Paul Rodzianko used to encourage a horse like this: to ensure that he came the right stride, a small fence about 3 ft (.9 m) or even less would be placed 22 ft (6.7 m) in front of a large fence of possibly 4 ft 6 in (1.4 m) or 5 ft (1.5 m). The rider could then ride fast at the small one, landing possibly 5 ft away, take one long non-jumping stride of about 12 ft (3.7 m) and then, having met the first right or wrong, he would certainly be right for the large fence. These fences always had good ground lines, and were so placed in order that the rider could carry out a figure of eight. This system not only gives the rider confidence but the horse too because it is obviously more difficult to judge the stride, when and where to take off when going at a fast canter and jumping larger fences for the first time.

This method may also be used to ensure your horse comes 'right' when learning to jump water, but in this case the fence of 3 ft (.9 m) or more should be placed at a distance of 29 ft (8.8 m) from the fence of the water. The horse will then, having landed over the first fence at about 5 ft (1.5 m) distance, take two non-jumping strides each of 12 ft (3.7 m) and arrive at the correct point of take off for the water, which is as close as possible to the take off fence of the water.

Of course there will be faults that must be corrected. The horse may not pick up his forelegs, but he'll soon learn to do so having hit the odd fence. You can put an inch (2.5 cm) thick length of old gas piping either over or in front of the fence—if hit it'll make a good deal of noise but will not harm the horse. Undoubtedly the most difficult fault to cure is 'refusing'. When a horse starts doing that the rider is usually to blame for asking too much of him. It might be necessary to go back to the beginning: only then can the horse regain his confidence.

[33]

CHAPTER VI

Progress

The two major factors in our training so far can be pin-pointed in the words 'obedience' and 'style'. The first was beautifully defined by Field Marshal Lord Wavell when he said to me once, 'a horse must learn to obey with the proud obedience of a soldier'. That is clear, but the question of 'style' is a little more difficult. Horses that jump in the *correct* style, using head and neck, rounding their back, will jump more easily and have a better chance of success. In general, that is.

1. Leopard, ridden by the author, demonstrates obedience.

2. Leopard, ridden by the author, demonstrates style and obedience without a bridle.

But of course I'm perfectly well aware that a horse may break all or many of the rules and still make a champion. Horses, like horsemen, have personalities. I think particularly of David Broome's Sunsalve (although I could never see him) which won us a bronze medal at the Rome Olympics in 1960. That horse jumped with a flat back and legs dangling, but David's knowledge of horsemanship told him not to try to change its style. He adapted his way of riding to help Sunsalve and won through.

David Broome is a really great horseman who has succeeded with many different horses. Nevertheless it's tantalizing to imagine what Sunsalve might have done had he learned to bascule correctly when young—as was the case with, say, Lt. Colonel Harry Llewellyn's Monty. One is always looking for the perfect animal. Could we combine Sunsalve's courage and jumping power with Monty's perfection of movement, what a horse we might have!

Perhaps the best horse I ever had, and certainly my best friend, was one, Leopard, who jumped in perfect style and always better without a bridle.

[35]

Commandant Lessage at the French Cavalry School, Saumur, taught me much. There I learned the supreme importance of the work on the flat, and the necessity of adapting to differences in a horse's personality.

Some horsemen believe that whatever the conformation of the horse, it must always be dominated and trained to approach and jump in exactly the same way. I believe it fair to say that in general it's the method of the German school. Hans Winkler, though, is a notable exception. Personally I think that, while striving to make the horse jump in the orthodox fashion, finally one must adapt to the essential nature of that horse's personality.

The next stage, then, is to train our horse to jump small, varied fences: we might even jump two, three or four in a straight line, or try a change of direction, but we won't be in a hurry to attempt a complete course.

By good fortune, when I became interested in show jumping I happened to be stationed at Aldershot. There we had an ideal training place, then known as the Mounted Sports Ground. It was a field of about six acres (2.4 h) with every type of fixed natural fence. Post and rails, ditches, railway crossings, and even railway lines with telephone or signal wires laid. Water jumps of all sizes, cut and laid hedges, the whole place surrounded by woods where you found perfect tracks. And everywhere an ideal, sandy going. Luckily for me there were also flat, empty spaces where artificial show jumps could be built as a course.

(On this very field our British team, under the captaincy of Lt. Colonel Harry Llewellyn—Wilf White, Lt. Colonel Duggie Stewart, Peter Robeson and the trainer, Lt. Colonel Jack Talbot Ponsonby—trained to win our first ever Gold Medal at the Helsinki Olympics in 1952.)

I particularly emphasize this Mounted Sports Ground, for it was the finest setting for the training of a show jumper, event horse or hunter I've ever known. And I was doubly lucky in having the help there of the finest instructor of this century. His name was Colonel Paul Rodzianko. He'd learnt the art and indeed necessity of dressage from James Fillis, chief instructor at the Russian Cavalry School, St. Petersburg. Incidentally, Fillis had been an instructor at Saumur—the only Englishman ever to hold such a post. But Paul Rodzianko wasn't content with dressage as a self-sufficient art—it had to have a purpose—so off he went to Italy to work with the great teacher in jumping, Caprilli.

[36]

3. Lt Col H. M. Llewellyn, G.B., on Monty—brilliant knee action and use of the head and neck.

To sum up, Aldershot provided me with one of those rare periods in life—unique conditions for making the best use of one's time.

The ground was about a mile from the barracks, so the horse had an opportunity to settle down on its way. Nevertheless when I got there I always spent at least ten minutes on the flat, 'suppling' my horse, as any athlete will before his race.

Now, as then, begins the real business of training my horse to jump fences he may meet in a horse show. Seven or eight fences will have been laid out, varied in colour and make up, with an emphasis on spread fences to extend the training of the correct style. Some might be in a line, but they won't necessarily be jumped as a definite course. That depends on what problems your horse raises.

To jump the fence properly, the horse must take off at the correct spot. It will be, as already stated, at a distance of between the height of the fence and plus a half away. So for a 4 ft (1.2 m) fence he should

[37]

take off somewhere between 4 ft and 6 ft (1.8 m). As the fence gets higher, he must take off nearer the inside limit of the zone i.e. for a 5 ft (1.5 m) fence it would be nearer 5 ft than 7 ft 6 ins (2.3 m).

However, the fences we're dealing with at this stage are not more than 3 ft 6 ins (1.1 m) high, and I jump them at a trot, not allowing my horse to anticipate and break into a canter as he approaches.

Don't jump the fences in any particular order, just quietly circle among them, always at the trot, and when you feel right for a particular fence, go straight on and jump it. We'll jump at the place I judge to be right, at the trot. If my horse canters, I quietly check him on the circle and bring him back to the trot.

Jumping, the rider must have a firm and independent seat so as not to lose contact with the horse's mouth. Legs must be kept in the same position, increasing the pressure as we approach the fence. At the take off, your horse must have complete freedom, although contact is maintained.

But however firm your seat, particularly at the trot, a rider may be left at the take off—so it's essential to have either a breast plate or neck strap to grab hold of.

An independent, strong seat can only be attained by endless exercises. The best thing is to ride and jump without stirrups. In pre-war days, it was the custom to teach young recruits to jump down lanes with no stirrups, arms folded in front. But this was wrong: arms should be folded behind, otherwise the rider's seat tends to move backwards. If the arms are held behind, the rider's back will be hollowed or remain straight, but never rounded. Similarly, when a ballet dancer jumps, his pelvis should be thrust forward, otherwise he loses the centre of balance.

When all's going well I might perhaps, after a walk, jump three or four fences as in a course, at a steady canter. Always insisting that whatever the fence my horse jumps it at the exact spot I intend, sometimes at an angle. For instance if the rider finds he's coming too close for the take off, he can by angling it get more room. This is also of great advantage in 'speed' competitions, though if you do it at a spread fence the size of the jump will of course be increased.

Naturally, things don't always go right and one of the worst problems is a refusal. When that happens I must immediately ask myself why. Perhaps the take off point chosen made it quite impossible for him to jump. Maybe he had become frightened and I was asking him too much. Anyway, the rider should hold him to the fence and

4. and 5. If the arms are folded behind the back, the back of the rider will
be hollowed or remain straight.

let him have a good look; then, having jumped another fence, bring him back to try again at the one he's refused. (You will remember this routine from the lunging chapter.) If he refuses a second time, he must be punished with the whip, still holding the horse to the fence. It should then be lowered and the horse made to jump it two or three times. Then raise it and jump again.

Perhaps when circling the horse may run out, but unless that becomes repetitious it's better it ignore it, or pretend to have meant it. Immediately attempt the fence again, your whip hand on the side he ran out. If he does it a second time, bring the whip down hard.

Throughout this training over small fences, work on the lunge should be continued so that if, for whatever reason, you are unable to ride your horse, he can then be lunged (but not ridden) over fences by a friend.

These days of early training are fun, and even if the horse doesn't have the ability to become a top class show jumper, always remember how much more pleasure you will both have hunting.

CHAPTER VII

The Decision Made: Now to Show Jump

We all ride for pleasure but that pleasure is much enhanced if we have a certain end in view. The object may be to train my horse so that he can pull out and jump a large fence to keep with hounds, or to have more fun 'eventing', or a win point-to-pointing.

Riding is an expensive sport, so the rider will always want to improve his technique and train his horse in order that, to put it bluntly, he gets his money's worth. And we all like the feeling of having achieved something.

In the past five chapters, I've endeavoured to explain a method of training a horse which would now be ready to go hunting, eventing or show jumping. In this case it will be the last, for I have no doubt at all that our horse is potentially a good show jumper! He is obedient, calm, jumps small fences in perfect style and we both *enjoy* jumping. He is now 5 or 6 years old and ready for the final training before his first show. I've purposely not used the word 'competing' as this first show will be part of his training programme.

I shall continue with a definite schedule for each day. If out of doors: a walk to the schooling ground, work on the flat for ten minutes, then small individual fences of which the majority will be parallel bars—to consolidate my horse's jumping in the correct style. (These single fences will seldom be over 3 ft 6 in (1.1 m).) At a trot, to begin with, then at the canter later in the lesson.

At least three times a week I should lay out a complete course of fences as varied as I can think of: among them the ordinary double oxers, parallel bars, the gate, a wall, perhaps a stile to test obedience. Each fence, particularly the first would have a good ground line, for

[41]

now I'm going to start jumping the course in the correct order and at a canter.

Were I lucky enough to be in our Mounted Sports Ground or its equivalent, I'd loosen my horse up on the flat and over two or three small fences before entering the area of the complete course. If the latter has, say, seven fences I shall jump the course twice.

Having entered, I canter two or three circles to let him have the feel of the ring, and when I feel he's ready, jump the first fence. This one will invariably be easy but fairly firmly fixed, so I can ride at it with confidence. Throughout the round I shall try to keep at the same pace: if I feel we're coming in at the wrong stride, I'll shorten or lengthen it from as far back as possible. The experienced rider will 'see' his stride i.e. know if he's coming right for the take off from some distance away.

Should the rider wish to shorten, he must sit still, and while maintaining impulsion with his legs increase the contact on the horse's mouth. On no account must this be a sudden pull, or the horse will raise his head. The greater the tension on the reins, the greater your pressure with both legs. If the stride has to be lengthened, you must ease the tension on the reins, still keeping contact, and increasing pressure with your legs.

Watching experienced riders from the ringside it will be seen that the horse will always appear to be going at much the same pace: if the speed or length of stride must be increased or diminished, it will be done with the smoothness of an expert driving a high powered motor car, no sudden acceleration or braking.

So, never hurry during the jumping of these small courses and always try to keep an even pace. Gradually introduce combinations of fences, doubles and trebles, but always at the correct distance—we'll come to that in a minute.

Probably much of this training will be done indoors, in which case loosen up your horse over two or three fences, and then go out of doors before entering to tackle the complete course.

At times it may be desirable to test the courage and ability of your horse to jump larger fences of 4 ft 6 in (1.4 m) or even 5 ft (1.5 m)—for obviously he will have to eventually. But it's important that they be put at a correct distance from the preceding fence so that your horse comes right. If he fails to jump one of these or refuses, remember the routine in the last chapter: lower the fence and jump it again so that he can regain his confidence.

6. Pat Smythe, G.B., on Tosca showing how water should be jumped—
superb extension.

I can't stress enough that these days of training must never become
monotonous to the horse. A quiet meander and work-out, and if
possible a hack in the countryside, should be cunningly interspersed
with the more exacting training. When schooling my polo ponies in
those days of grass we'd find a field where I could canter in circles,
over ridge and furrow, or on a slope, and that helped to balance my
pony and 'muscle' him up.

But to get back to our rider. When we now jump a definite course
of seven or eight fences, he should decide on the track he intends to
take, and, to contrive a longer course, the second part should follow a
different track.

The question of distances: at the outset it's better that each fence
should be dissociated from the others, and not depend on the previous
fence to enable you to come 'right' for the one that follows. Therefore,
to begin with, all fences should be at least 80 ft (24.4 m) apart. As we
progress, distances will be shortened, and then it's up to the rider to

determine his approach to the correct point of take off—whether to shorten or lengthen a stride. And you must make up your mind well before the last three or four strides; it's a mistake at the last two or three strides to realize one is wrong, and either rush or pull back.

Still, there'll be occasions when the horse will take off too close, or too far; it can't always be avoided. So the rider must adapt himself. If too close, he must continue pressing with his legs while retaining even more contact with the horse's mouth. On the other hand, when the horse stands back, although maintaining pressure with your legs, open your fingers and allow the reins to slide. Never hang on and cause the horse to be jabbed in the mouth: this will raise his head, causing him to flatten his back and drop the hind legs.

During these weeks fences can easily be varied by placing bales of straw, bundles of faggots, angling the poles and so on. Your horse will become used to every type, shape and colour that he's likely to encounter in the ring.

Above all you must concentrate on the bond of obedience, confidence and sympathy between horse and rider. Obedience plainly means the horse must jump at the required time and place, but it's the responsibility of the rider to bring him to a particular spot. And

7. Bill Steinkraus, U.S.A., on Sinjon—jumping a double oxer.

8. Commandant Bill Ringrose, Ireland, riding Loch an Espaig at Ostend.

you must grow close to your horse so that you can shorten or lengthen his stride without disturbing the steady cadence or rhythm.

As the time approaches for our first trial, remember that it's the rider, not the horse, who is sitting the examination. It follows that he must select this first show with some care. Maybe it would be good to let your horse meet the excitement of a crowd at a one day event with fixed fences. Possibly it might be better just to take him along: we won't compete, but allow him to move about and become accustomed to the excitement, bustle and colour of a show ground.

During the last days of preparation don't change your normal routine except, perhaps, if you have a friend not too far away, it would be good experience for your horse to put him in the horse-box and take him to jump in a strange ring or school. This can also give him a rehearsal for 'boxing'.

Now the rider must try to think of every detail and possible con-

[45]

tingency. Has your horse been really well shod? Has he screws, if the ground should prove slippery? A mackintosh sheet in case of pouring rain? Have you a pair of string gloves? Are there bandages for the legs when travelling? A head guard lest the horse jerk his head up on the move? A tail guard? Has the saddlery been checked?

During these chapters I've tried to put down my thoughts on the training of a horse—when all goes right and one has sufficient time. For I can assure potential trainers there are no short cuts if perfection, or near perfection, is your goal. I've tried to itemize the likely problems: refusing, running out, dropping a leg from pure careless-ness! These faults can and must be corrected. I'll emphasize again that the careless knocking down of fences is usually amended by placing a light gas pipe either before or on top of the fence; this should be varied over the course. If that doesn't suffice you must ride your horse over fixed fences, but on no account go back to the old methods of 'rapping'. 'Tack poles', or rapping with a pole, are not now necessary. Present day fences being solid in appearance, your horse will jump them, if he's properly trained and you ride him correctly.

There are the odd occasions when a horse must be punished for disobedience. If you have to do that, don't let it be when you're on a tarmac road. Wait till he repeats the crime in a ploughed field, let the lesson be sharp, and then forget about it.

Whyte Melville once wrote, 'the great horseman must give an inch to take a mile'. That's an excellent guide line not only for the training of a horse, but for the whole of one's life.

CHAPTER VIII

Walking the Course

The great day arrives, and whether you're introducing a young horse to his first minor show or jumping an experienced one at an international affair, your feelings and procedures will be much the same.

The onus is on the rider. Have you picked the right time and venue? If it's a young horse, the one we've been training, try to choose a show where you're certain the fences will be well built, and preferably a two-day one so that he gradually becomes accustomed to his lively surroundings, the spectators, tents, his fellow competitors, possibly even a band.

In the army I luckily had the opportunity with my 'Trick Ride' to take along spare horses to various shows. They wouldn't be required to enter the ring, but as potential young jumpers they could start to scent the atmosphere, so that in future all the pageantry wouldn't distract them from the job in hand.

With both beginners and experienced horses there'll be many competitions where you jump for experience but not necessarily to win. The rider must wait and watch for the time when he *can* push his horse to the maximum effort.

Writing this I think of two outstandingly great horsemen, Peter Robeson of Great Britain and Bill Steinkraus of the U.S.A. Both Olympic medallists (Bill Steinkraus won an Individual Gold at Mexico in 1968, Peter a Bronze in 1956 at Stockholm and again at Tokyo in 1964), neither of these perfectionists has ever been in a hurry to achieve a win. To train their horses correctly, that's all that matters to them, so that the horse will be right on the big day of their choosing.

9. Lt Col H. M. Llewellyn, G.B., on Foxhunter, clinches the Team Gold
Medal at Helsinki, 1952. A triple of brush—a staircase fence.

Harry Llewellyn, an Olympic Gold Medallist in 1952, was always
patient because he'd learnt from experience that one simply had to be.
He was supreme in the show jumping arena, but also as an amateur
steeplechase rider. At the Cheltenham meeting in 1948 he won the
National Hunt Foxhunters on State Control, quickly followed by the
United Hunts on Bay Marble; both horses owned, trained and ridden
by himself—a performance never equalled. And to emphasize proof of
his great ability, that same year he rode Foxhunter to help win a
bronze for us at the Olympics, then a week later won the King George
V at the Royal International Horse Show. A great 'all rounder', for
he'd ridden Ego into second place in the 1936 Grand National and was
fourth the following year.

Captain Piero d'Inzeo, another great all rounder, won steeplechases
in Italy and rode in the 1948 Olympic Three Day Event at Aldershot.

[48]

There's Fritz Thiedermann of Germany who at the 1952 Olympics competed in the Grand Prix de Dressage as well as the show jumping; and of course Hans Winkler, who has won more Olympic Gold Medals than any other horseman in the world. He understands how to be patient and bide his time.

I know that all the great names would agree on this point. I think of those who came to the fore in Britain, with three or more horses, who were prepared to wait for just the right moment to go for a big win. Pat Smythe, now Mrs Koechlin-Smythe, was responsible for putting the Horse of the Year Show on the map in 1949, by winning the Leading Show Jumper of the Year on Finality. She was the first woman to win an Olympic Show Jumping medal, riding Flanagan with the British Team that won the Bronze in 1956. Who will ever forget her successes on Prince Hal, Tosca, Scorchin?

David Broome, possibly the greatest show jumper in the world at the present time, has won the European Championship on three occasions (once on Sunsalve and twice on Mister Softee), and the World Championship on Beethoven in 1970. He, like Harry Llewellyn, Bill Steinkraus and Piero d'Inzeo, has won the King George V Gold

10. David Broome, G.B., a World and European Champion, on Sunsalve— over a curved wall.

11. Bill Steinkraus, U.S.A., riding Snowbound. Hardly surprising that this great pair should win the Individual Gold Medal at Mexico, 1968.

Trophy three times since the war.

These riders, and I've only mentioned a few, never fail to attend to every detail when introducing a young horse to his first show—or indeed at any other time.

Always be sure to arrive early, to ease your horse into the atmosphere. But under international rules a horse must never be taken into the ring before competing.

The rider should study in advance the conditions on the programme. It will show the number of jumps-off and the speed required. A course plan will always be posted up at least an hour before the start. You must memorize that, if you can, before walking the course—for which you'll only get five or ten minutes at many shows. On the continent where they have nothing but jumping classes the time may be unlimited, but here and in the U.S.A. the ring is used for other classes such as hunters, hacks or harness. And an indoor show like Wembley works to a tight schedule.

At Rome and Lucerne a course builder can spend all morning at his ask: I've spent many a happy hour learning from Colonel Haccius, he greatest of all in that field. However, Alan Ball when building at Wembley, Mrs Pamela Carruthers in New York, or even Mickey Brinckmann, are often pressed for time and their planning has to be all the more immaculate.

In my day I often used to walk around with Colonel Dan Corry who is so knowledgable. He would advise generally, not going into measurements, more like walking a point-to-point course. But now as in every sport we've become thoroughly specialized and no detail can be ignored or skimped. Twenty years ago the 1500 metres was run in about 4 minutes; today 3 minutes 32.2 seconds. Standards in our sport have similarly risen.

Given the signal to enter the arena, we study the approach to the start and the first fence: is it fairly solid, will it take a knock, can one ride at it with confidence? On to the second fence, and if it's within distance of about 72 ft (22 m) the rider will carefully pace the distance. The whys and wherefores of this are explained in chapter 13. The thing is to calculate where your horse will land, and you'll know that in good going the average stride of the horse, moving at about 383 yards (350 m) per minute, will be between 11 ft 6 in (3.5 m) and 12 ft (3.7 m). If we take the average rider's pacing as 3 ft (.9 m), that means four paces to one stride of his horse. Therefore if he paces five of the horse's strides from the last place of landing and finds he's standing about right for the next take off, he'll be well satisfied. That should bring him to about 5 ft (1.5 m) or 6 ft (1.8 m) from the next fence. If it only brings you to, say, 8 ft (2.4 m) away, you'll have to make up your mind either to lengthen one or two strides after landing, and still use the five strides, or to shorten a couple of strides and so jump after putting in an extra one.

At each fence, the same drill. Is it fairly firm? Or will it fall at a touch? Must it be jumped at any particular spot, or perhaps at an angle?

If possible take a look at the shorter course for the jump-off, in case you're fortunate enough to get a clear round.

Some riders make short notes, others think it unnecessary.

Even when I was jumping, although not so concerned with distances I always studied the course well, in order not to have to think of the track. Having walked it, I'd sit down and think: Through the start, take the first fence at a good pace, that's easy and firm. Give myself enough room for the second fence and ride on at it, for it's a large

[51]

spread. Now take a short stride and steady as this is a gate demanding obedience and accuracy, then a right turn, taking plenty of room as the next is a parallel bars, quickly followed by the double which Dan assures me will ride right, provided I ride on at it. . . .

Having memorized the course like that I felt fairly safe, and at least sure that I wouldn't lose my way!

Nowadays, as Director of the two London shows I stand in the ring when the riders go through this ritual, pacing every distance and checking the solidity of each fence. Perhaps one day computers may be used but even they make mistakes, and everything can go wrong if a horse pecks on landing, or shortens his stride during the approach after taking an extra look at the fence. It's then that a great rider such as Harvey Smith comes into his own. Incidentally, I may be wrong but I think he doesn't worry about long distances, although he carefully studies them in the combinations—where he can make up time by a short turn, etc.

Some of these riders—Harvey Smith, David Broome or Hans Winkler—walk the course on their own, thinking hard. Others go around as a team with their Chef d'Equipe, such as Bert de Nemethy of the U.S.A., one of the finest of all trainers, or the German team with their charming expert, Gustav Pfordte.

12. Peter Robeson, G.B., another great perfectionist, riding Firecrest at Rotterdam—over an unusual rustic oxer.

13. Captain Piero d'Inzeo, Italy, on Sunbeam, jumping parallel bars at the Royal International Horse Show. Piero d'Inzeo has won the King George V Cup on three occasions.

I stand and listen, knowing they don't want to be distracted. When he bell rings the riders must leave the arena. Those who jump early n·the draw are a little unfortunate for they won't see from others 1ow the course rides. Hence the rotation in international competi-ions.

Before being called, ride your horse in for five or ten minutes, more f necessary, then jump the practice fence in the collecting ring. On 10 account will you be allowed to alter the character of this fence, or ;et some friend to 'rap' the horse.

Those jumping later will be sitting in groups with their expert dvisers—in our case Harry Llewellyn or Ronnie Massarella—but ome, Harvey Smith for instance, prefer to concentrate and watch ·very movement by themselves. Then they too will leave to loosen up heir horses.

On entering, the rider must remember to salute the judges and hen will have a trot or canter round, but he mustn't show his horse any fence. If it's Harvey Smith or David Broome he'll possibly be looking to make sure some particular pole has been put back in the cup correctly. And why not? Think of the famous cricketer who comes out to pat down some blemish in the seemingly immaculate turf. Hans Winkler or Alwin Schockemöhle will be reining their horses back, getting them really supple and well on the bit. When the bell rings, you must go through the start within a minute of it sounding. No more warming up or patting down the pitch. . . .

I cannot believe there's any great rider who's not nervous—or 'windy' as I call it. He may not show it, but without nerves he can hardly rise to the great occasion. That's why walking the course is so important: knowing when to turn, whether to shorten a stride, or to cut in at an angle and thus save time. A big competition is rarely won unless some risk is taken. When it comes off, everyone in the stand will say 'Goodness, what superb riding'; if it fails, the same spectators will say, 'How stupid to expect his horse to do that!' One of the minor injustices of life.

Few will forget Paddy McMahon on Penwood Forgemill winning the Victor Ludorum at the Horse of the Year Show, when he defeated Paul Schockemöhle, riding Abadir, by one tenth of a second. That means that had they been racing or jumping together there would have been a mere eighteen inches between them.

More extraordinary still: after a clear round in the jump-off for the Queen Elizabeth II Cup, Ann Moore, riding her father's horse Psalm and Alison Dawes on Mr Banbury both clocked the same time to 1/10th of a second. At the Horse of the Year Show, Ann Moore, again with Psalm, did exactly the same thing against David Broome riding Sportsman—on two separate occasions, 1971 and 1973, in the same competition!

You will hardly need further proof that time spent on reconnaissance is never wasted. With a young or even an experienced horse, always walk the course carefully, and then watch like an eagle those experts competing against you. If you only save a yard in your track it can easily mean the difference between losing and winning.

CHAPTER IX

Arranging a Horse Show

There are thousands of shows now all over the world, and although many may be small (both indoor and outdoor) these are the veins and blood vessels which keep the sport of show jumping alive. They nurture the riders and horses of the future. Moreover, the bigger shows should be in, or get themselves into, a position where they can help to subsidize those smaller ones, as is the case with our own major event, The Horse of the Year Show in London, which has been able to subsidize less fortunate concerns—providing for the hiring of jumps, timing equipment and of course a general fund of acquired knowledge.

The appetite of both rider and spectator will be whetted if these small shows are well organized and presented. That organization will guarantee that your riders and the public become increasingly interested and involved in the sport in the years to come. There is a strong market element here and every committee should remember that it must give something worth while for its money; few people now wish to support an enterprise that's not succeeding. The days of fairy godfathers—those benevolent vice presidents ready to foot the bill of your losses—they've gone for ever, and their place has been taken by commercial firms who are quite ready to sponsor you provided you have the makings of success.

Success, what does that entail? Competitors *must* enjoy themselves. It must be clear to them that your aim is to encourage better horsemanship and horsemastership, to ensure that the better types of horse will be bred. But above all you must give pleasure to the spectator, whether or not he is knowledgeable about horses.

To succeed, the show must have perfect timing, endless variety,

15. Kathy Kusner, U.S.A., on Aberali, jumping the great wall at Aachen
using a bitless bridle.

imaginative production. The machinery will not run smoothly unless there's a happy understanding between exhibitors, competitors and the officials and stewards.

I honestly think the principles of organization remain the same, whether your show be grand and international or small and local. There will be variations of detail, naturally, but even as between indoor and outdoor events the principles are constant.

Dates are a primary consideration and wherever possible should be made easy for competitors (not sensible for either riders or horses to travel miles unnecessarily), and this is why, for instance, the All England Jumping Show at Hickstead usually precedes the Royal International Horse Show at Wembley, which in turn is followed by Dublin. Similarly Nice arranges its dates to precede Rome, and so on.

14. The arena at Wembley—the perfect indoor setting for the
Royal International Horse Show.

Most shows in the very full calendar have now established their venues. When choosing a site, a large area is essential for the parking of horse boxes and caravans; it should if possible have a ring for preliminary judging in addition to the main ring, and two collecting rings. The outside or practice ring should ideally be 80 yds (73.2 m) by 40 yds (36.6 m). Then you should have a pocket, or collecting ring, where the competitor waits while one or possibly two horses ahead jump.

Apart from the necessary area, your venue must have good exits and entrances. This is imperative for the smaller show—there's nothing more irritating than being halted in a queue for minutes on end, particularly with a horse box.

If the show's held out of doors, a main ring should be at least 120 yds (110 m) long by 80 yds wide. Indoors I think the ideal is 80 yds long by 40 yds wide.

Just before the last war I had the good fortune to direct a small show, and for the past twenty-five years or more I've had the privilege of producing both the Royal International and the Horse of the Year Shows. Until 1967 the former was held out of doors, first at the White City, then in the outdoor stadium at Wembley, and finally indoors there. The Horse of the Year Show has always been staged indoors, but in or out, I repeat, the principles remain the same: enjoyment for riders and owners, excitement and variety for the spectator and, never forget, the show must pay its way.

In many respects I think it's easier to produce a show indoors, although against that it means you have to maintain a much faster pace, with your timing meticulously exact and all that it involves. But at least there are no worries about the weather—rain brings you unending problems.

Let us do a dummy run of the prospective director discussing his programme with the committee. Beforehand I try to visualize what the competitor will expect and the spectator would wish to watch. Variety there must be, obviously, and you endeavour to establish a rhythm. There can't be unceasing climaxes, so a round of excitement will perhaps be followed by a 'Show' class being finally judged—in that way the audience has a chance to relax. Inevitably that means either two rings or time in the main ring for the preliminary judging of show and even jumping classes. Some exhibitors or competitors may be impatient of this preliminary judging, but having to keep your eyes glued on endless jumping, or watch the tails of show horses while

16. Hans Winkler, Germany, on Halla, with whom he won the Individual Gold Medal in the 1956 Olympics. In all Hans Winkler has won five Gold Medals.

judges 'ride' each horse for three or four minutes, spinning the class out to an hour or more, both are equally ruinous to a performance. In most cases a jumping class shouldn't last more than fifty to seventy minutes in the main ring, and the final judging of a show class should be completed in ten to fifteen minutes.

Certainly there will always be those experts who wish to study closely the conformation of every horse, but the time for that is at the preliminary judging. If your show is to succeed, the supporter who really matters is a man who brings his wife and two or three children: they come for excitement and won't do so again unless there's variety, with the whole thing planned and run to time.

I'll give my most careful thought to the jumping competitions. A rider may perhaps have brought three horses: consequently there must be three or four classes in the day to enable him to jump one horse in each of them. But it's wrong to allow him to jump two or three horses in a major competition—plainly it gives him too great an advantage over those with only one. These jumping classes on the

17. Iris Kellett of Ireland, Ladies European Champion in 1969, riding
Morning Light at Ostend.

same day will have variations in their conditions: e.g. one for the
young horse only, perhaps a speed competition, and of course the
major event with one or two jumps-off.

I believe there can be too much emphasis on speed. In France after
the last war, there were few competitions where speed wasn't encouraged during the very first round, therefore the emphasis was on
speed, and not jumping.

Well now, having sorted out the jumping competitions we must
consider the show and harness classes. To help the owners and avoid
congestion with stabling, I'll arrange the hunter classes on possibly
two days and the show ponies on another couple of days. All this part
of the planning must be done about nine months before the show, and
when the main structure is settled I then decide what displays we
need to add to the entertainment.

We're very fortunate in this country because we still breed so many
different types of horse; our hackneys are superb in the driving classes.

Displays of Dressage and Musical Rides can be very costly; they don't attract the public unless really exceptional and of something like world wide fame. Examples are Olympic Gold Medallists in Dressage, possibly the 'Sherry' horses of recent years, the Spanish Riding School, the Cadre Noir from Saumur, and certainly the Hungarian Herdsmen.

The best drawing displays are competitive ones such as we've built up here, particularly at the Horse of the Year Show. The Mounted Games attracts an entry of 180 teams each year and the last night of that championship resembles a Cup Tie—but no rough stuff or unpleasantness. The Quadrille of the Year in which our riding clubs take part is quite superb, the 'Ride and Drive' event equally exciting, and increasingly we have driving competitions.

These ingredients will give you quite enough variety for, after all, horse shows aren't pageants, and even out of doors I don't think a producer need rely on flag throwing in a gale at an agricultural show, or parachutists, or motor cyclists ploughing through mud to the accompaniment of banging drums which split in the rain!

So all this we will have worked out before presenting our plan to the committee, together with a careful budget of income and expenditure, guided by my highly efficient Secretary, George Worboys. With the help of sponsors I'll endeavour to make a profit, for unless I do, the future of our show will be limited. A schedule is then prepared giving precise conditions but no 'timings'—these must wait until I know the exact number of entries. At the same time I plan the flowers, hotel accommodation, the amount of stabling required. For the Horse of the Year Show I'll require over 500 loose boxes.

The schedule has now gone to press and our first phase completed!

CHAPTER X

Planning the Attack

Should your show be held out of doors it's as well to leave a track of some 30–40 ft (9–12 m) around the jumping courses. This will enable the course builder to make his changes unobtrusively for the next competition, whilst harness or show classes are being judged on that outside track.

If you're indoors, it's undoubtedly best always to start with jumping: the course is ready set and competitors and judges have had the opportunity to inspect or walk the course beforehand. When you come to the second jumping competition, I've learned from experience that this should be the last class and there must be a definite interval of 20 minutes in which to build that course and allow competitors to walk it. This is when the band comes into its own and the public also has the opportunity of visiting the trade stands.

At my London shows, whether indoor or outdoor, there is always what I term Control or Battle HQ. This is positioned at a central point and in the case of the Empire Pool at Wembley is at the ringside with easy access to the arena. There, the television commentator sits with a monitor set alongside so that I, or John Stevens the assistant director, know exactly what is going out: nearby sits a steward in charge of the public address with, on his right, another senior steward who's connected by telephone to the collecting ring, the judges and the electric scoreboard. Behind these three or four (there's usually a reserve) sit two more stewards who are watching the time: Is this class going to finish late? By how much? Is it going to finish early?—if so the collecting rings must be warned.

18. 'Control' in action.

I nearly always stand behind control and am fully informed by just listening. If my timing's being put out I have to decide with the judges whether a 'standard' should be introduced. This may be brought in if a competitor has too many faults to be placed in the awards. For example, should there be seven awards, and you already have three competitors without faults, and five with 4, any rider making more than 4 faults may be retired to save precious minutes.

There should be four judges at an International Show, including at least one from another country. This neutral judge, as we'll call him, sits behind the other three, and he is responsible for the International Federation Rules being strictly upheld. The time-keeper sits with the judges. Normally at these major shows there'll be a digit clock, which is started when the rider passes through a ray and stopped when he finishes through another; when it stops, the clock stamps the rider's time and a judge writes the competitor's number on the back of the card.

On the right of control sit the honorary veterinary surgeon and the honorary medical officer, with another veterinary surgeon in the outside ring where a horse ambulance stands by, near the farrier. A stretcher party sits near the entrance. The arena party is also drilled in case of any accident to a horse, and screens provided should it be necessary to destroy one. (I haven't had to do that once in twenty-five years and whenever the thought crosses my mind I still touch my pipe or any bit of wood within reach.)

19. Lt Col U. Mariles Cortes, Mexico, riding Arete in the 1948 Olympics in London, jumping the last fence to win the Individual and Team Gold Medal.

In addition to the show jumping classes there are the show hunter, hack and harness classes. These classes are run by a separate team of stewards under a senior steward.

When jumping is taking place, the collecting ring is managed by one of the senior stewards and four others, two of whom are in the outside collecting ring and two in the inside collecting ring. Those in the outside collecting ring not only call the competitors but make sure the practise fences are only jumped in the right direction and that the rules prohibiting cruelty are strictly observed. Another senior steward outside acts as stable manager, allocating the stabling and watchful that the fire regulations are strictly enforced. Then there are additional stewards to look after the guests in the Royal Box and to entertain our sponsors.

But to step back a little way in the sequence of preparations, as soon as the schedule is drafted, the course builder receives a copy specifying conditions for every competition. He must have ample time, for once his designs are ready at least eight photostats will be made before the rush of entries begins. One copy for the judges, one for the collecting ring board, one for a board now placed at the entry to the arena—that a rider in any doubt may have one last look before he jumps.

Every detail must be pondered during this slack period before entries start coming in. But slack has no meaning if you want your show, large or small, to be really great, not merely successful. For about three or four months before an opening I receive weekly advance booking figures, which I study carefully. Why is Thursday night down? Perhaps a world football tie falls on that day, if so, how can I counter it? No, if you look at it right, there's never a dull moment organizing a show.

If an affair of this kind fails, it's customary to blame either the public relations officer or the weather. Publicity is important and I personally find it is absolutely essential to work closely with my P.R.O. The director of a small show may say that it doesn't matter to them— they cannot afford such luxuries as a P.R.O. . . . Frankly that is rubbish. An enthusiastic organizer who demonstrates that he knows his job can always get voluntary help.

Everything in life—and I've said it often—is TIMING. The first phase of the attack is to make sure that the club members (in the case of the two London shows) are circulated: the sooner subscriptions are renewed and fresh people encouraged to join, the better. Then the organizer will know what proportion of income can be expected from

20. Nelson Pessoa, Brazil, on Nagir in superb harmony.

this source. Publicity is entirely a matter of timing. Once your attack has begun the momentum must be sustained right up to the opening of the show.

Attention to detail spells out the difference between a good and bad production and if the production is known to be good the competitors will come. As simple as that. Then the spectators will come to see the competitors you've attracted, and the money they bring will enable you to increase lures to competitors and owners. The advantage will eventually seep back to the breeder, on whom standards ultimately depend.

Constantly I ask myself the following questions:

What are the advance booking figures? How do they compare with last year?

What are the entries, not only in the jumping classes but in the show classes?

What are the membership figures running at?

Which well known riders will be competing? Has my P.R.O. been told? Is he making the best use of these names?

Have I done everything to ensure that those who generously help me with sponsorship are being thanked?

Have I the best stewards available and do they realize they must somehow both uphold the rules and help the riders in every way possible, always remembering the riders are on edge before a competition?

As I sit in the train from Exeter to London I search my mind for things I may have forgotten, and always I keep checking the estimates of expenditure—hoping my estimate of income is conservative!

After the closing date of entries, the work for my small but highly efficient staff increases. I suppose in time we may come to use computers: and then perhaps as many mistakes will be found as in one's own bank statements.

Every entry form is carefully checked particularly with show jumpers, to be certain that horse and rider are eligible. Each entry is then recorded on two cards. One is filed in the classes for which that horse is eligible, for use in the programme, the second is filed in the general index of jumpers, from which the order of jumping will be drawn. As soon as the draw has been listed the second card is placed in the correct order for the programme.

21. Marion Coakes, G.B., rose to the top with her pony Stroller, because in spite of his size he jumped superbly in perfect style. This pair won the Ladies World Championship in 1966 at Hickstead and the Individual Olympic Silver Medal in Mexico in 1968.

The order of jumping is of great importance, especially in speed competitions for it may be an advantage to be drawn late. If, say, a hundred horses are entered, and if the show offers ten competitions, then the jumping order will be rotated by ten, that is to say that after the first competition the bottom ten horses in the draw are moved up to the top and so on for every competition.

Now that we have all the entries it's my job to draw up the final programme and, even more important, the timetable. As we carefully scrutinize the entries in each jumping class, it's not easy to decide how many will actually compete on the day, for a horse will quite likely be entered in two or three classes on that one day. From experience over many years we can make a fair estimate.

If I find that a class seems likely to contain forty or even fifty starters we may break it into sections. There are few things more tedious than watching from thirty to thirty-five horses competing in one event.

Now I make my notes according to the conditions of the class. Should there be one jump off against the clock, I decide how many clear rounds I would wish for. Usually one in five. Therefore, if I estimate there will be twenty-five to jump in the first round, then I hope for one in five of these to go clear to jump again in the second round; I will then have a total of thirty rounds.

At every show I should know pretty accurately how long each horse will take, according to the length of the course. In recent years when both the Royal International and the Horse of the Years Shows have been indoors at Wembley, I calculate that each round should take 1 minute 50 seconds, and allowing a further 5 minutes for the presentation of awards or change of course, I feel fairly safe. But there is inevitably a large number of variables and my highly efficient secretary Sally has to type out extensive notes, helped by Caroline (equally efficient), as I calculate the final timings. Needless to say these notes do not appear in the programme.

If I have any serious doubts, caution prevails, and I endeavour to finish early. Nothing that is good should ever go on too long.

Alas, one can never allow oneself to drift off into dreams, where just by being optimistic things always seem to come out right. They do not do so.

CHAPTER XI

On with the Show

Out of doors, owing to the vagaries of the weather, one of my constant headaches will obviously be the condition of the ground. Have I sufficient sand to put down if it's too dry, or wet—we won't talk about cloudbursts. Indoors, I find the best floor should have a basis of 4–5 inches of loam, not too wet, rolled very tight—in fact as hard as you can get it. On top of this should be laid a mixture of $\frac{1}{3}$ sand, $\frac{1}{3}$ sieved loam, and $\frac{1}{3}$ sawdust. Sometimes my contractor adds 5 cwt of salt to keep the top damped down.

A multitude of fiddling details revolves in my head during the last few days before the opening: Have I checked on the people who are to present the cups?—indeed have they been invited? Have all my sponsors been given parking space for VIPs in what we hope will be a crowded car park? That sort of thing. Early in the morning I wander around the stables, the preliminary judging rings, the car parks. It's simply incredible how, if you cannot see, you are bound to kick the only Coca-Cola tin within—well I was going to say within sight! I must say they do make a very disagreeable noise. Yet I've been fortunate; our grounds are usually so clean and tidy.

For a large show to run on time it's imperative to know first thing on each day the number of starters there will be in each jumping competition. So, by 10 am I shall have been given the exact number of riders who have declared to start and I carefully study the notes and estimates made when preparing my final time table. I always plan backwards from the time I intend to finish the evening performance: here perhaps I find that I'd allowed for twenty-five starters, hoping that the course built would get five horses clear for the first and only

[69]

jump-off. Alas, my calculation of the number of starters is out by five, which means I shall need another 9 minutes for this competition, even if everything else goes well. From there I work back through the time table to find I shall run, say, 10 minutes early. In that case I don't worry much and don't even try to slow the show down. It's a golden rule always to run at a fast pace for something else might go wrong—possibly a smashed obstacle—which will delay the whole evening. But if from the available evidence I find I'm going to be running 10 minutes late I decide to do something drastic, saving 2 or 3 minutes here and there on certain classes, or even starting the performance 10 minutes early. I warn the Director of Music, and the customers aren't cheated!

Sally, my personal secretary, types these final instructions straight down and they're ready for our conference, held each morning at 12 noon. Everyone with any responsibility attends this: every senior steward, the medical officer, the veterinary surgeon, the BBC producer, the commentator, the PA expert, the course builder, the senior judge, the musical director. When the instructions are handed round

22. Alwin Schockemohle, Germany, riding Donald Rex over the water at Hickstead. He was a member of the victorious German team in the 1960 Olympics.

they are read carefully, and comments don't lack humour, as you can imagine—that ingredient is vital, particularly towards the end of a long show when everyone's getting tired.

Of course we rehearse hard over several days before the opening, but to give you an idea of exactly what is involved, here are the instructions of the day for the dress rehearsal and a specimen performance.

2.00 pm DRESS REHEARSAL

Band will commence playing under the Direction of Major W. ALLEN. Scoreboard in operation. Telephones and Public Address checked and manned. Medical Officer and Veterinary Surgeon at control. All stewards to be on duty. Judges in Judges' Box. Spots not required.

Two Junior Leaders to report to Maj. F. BIRCHALL, for Scales. Maj. BIRCHALL will detail 2 Junior Leaders to open and shut gates under instructions from Mr R. PRIDE. Always correctly dressed, with No. 1 Dress Caps.

2.15 pm Arena Party will march to the centre of arena, as instructed by Maj. BIRCHALL. Mr D. WILLIAMS will announce the opening of the Show. Lights up. The first horse will be announced and the Ring Guard will sound. First horse sent in. Imaginary scores will be announced and scoreboard used. At conclusion, centre of Arena will be cleared, tractors used and pulled to one side. Awards sent in. Tractors exit. Awards formed up Mr D. BOURNE responsible. Presentation made. Outside fences removed. Awards sent out. Lap of Honour for Winner.

2.30 pm HEAVY HORSES

2.40 pm Lay out the course for ELDONIAN DOUBLE HARNESS STAKES. Mr BLACK, Mr HAYDON and Maj. BIRCHALL with 8 Arena Party to be responsible.

Mr PRIDE to arrange Collecting Ring Stewards.

Mr B. MILLS to be ready in Judges' Box.

2.45 pm CLASS 15: ELDONIAN DOUBLE HARNESS STAKES—

Section A (QUALIFYING ROUND)

The first six will qualify for the evening performance. One extra prize of £5 will be added to the Prize Money, so that all six competing in the evening performance will receive a prize. Estimate 12 to start. Allow 45 minutes, including removal of course.

[71]

3.30 pm PONY CLUB MOUNTED GAMES REHEARSAL
Mr R. BROOKS-WARD responsible.

3.45 pm PARADE OF PERSONALITIES—Dress to be worn.

4.00 pm Course for the BUTLIN CHAMPIONSHIP to be built.
IMMEDIATELY AFTER THE DRESS REHEARS-
AL the following will report to Colonel Sir Michael
ANSELL in the Conference Room:—Mr D. WILLIAMS,
Mr J. STEVENS, Mr B. PRIDE, Mr R. PRIDE, Mr R.
BROOKS-WARD, Mr M. BULLEN, Mr D. COLTON, Mr S.
HIGNETT, Maj. W. ALLEN, Mr R. HAYTER, and Wembley
Staff as directed by Mr G. STANTON.

4.20 pm Competitors in the Butlin Championship may walk the
course.

4.45 pm CLASS 20: THE BUTLIN CHAMPIONSHIP—Section I. Estimate 20 starters. Would like five clear rounds.
Course not too big. Owing to entries there will be three sections
and not two as in schedule.

5.30 pm CLASS 20: THE BUTLIN CHAMPIONSHIP—Section II Same as Section I.

6.15 pm The course to be changed for CLASS 19—THE LONDON
PALLADIUM.
Arena to be harrowed and raked.

6.30 pm Competitors in the London Palladium may walk the course.

THE HORSE OF THE YEAR SHOW 1973
October 8th–13th
INSTRUCTION NO. 2 GALA PERFORMANCE
MONDAY, 8th OCTOBER

6.40 pm The Band of the Royal Corps of Transport will commence
playing.

6.55 pm Arena Party form up to march in. Judges ready. All telephones and scoreboard manned. Mr C. HALL responsible.

6.57 pm Arena Party march in and form up in centre. 'Greensleeves'.
Mr D. WILLIAMS announces the opening of the 25th
Horse of the Year Show and the Gala Performance for the
Army Benevolent Fund, Riding for the Disabled, the
Injured Jockeys Fund and other Charities. Lights up. Arena
Party march to corners. First three to jump ready in inside
Collecting Ring. Mr R. PRIDE responsible.

7.00 pm CLASS 19: THE LONDON PALLADIUM CHAMP-
IONSHIP—Estimate 18 to start. Ring Guard to sound.
First horse to enter. Would like 5 clear for one jump-off.
Complete first round by 7.40 pm. Complete second round
with presentation by 7.50 pm. Before presentation the centre
of arena will be cleared. Band to play. Awards formed up.
Tractors to pull to one side. Awards enter. Mr PRIDE and
Mr BALL responsible. Trophy to be presented by Mr R. S.
SWIFT, General Manager, Moss Empires. Band will play.
Awards out. Lap of honour for winner.

7.50 pm HEAVY HORSES

8.00 pm CLASS 15: ELDONIAN DOUBLE HARNESS
STAKES—Section A, Mr BLACK as already rehearsed will
lay out the course. Mr R. BROOKS-WARD will com-
mentate as briefed. 6 starters. All to receive prizes and
rosettes. Mr J. STEVENS responsible for lining up awards.
Awards will be presented by . . . .

8.25 pm BUTLIN MOUNTED GAMES COMPETITION—
All six teams competing.

8.45 pm HORSE PERSONALITIES

9.05 pm INTERVAL—Band will be announced and spotted. Selec-
tions from 'The King and I'.

9.25 pm CLASS 20: THE BUTLIN CHAMPIONSHIP—Sec-
tion III & Final
Estimate 20 starters. Allow with presentation and changing
of course for final, 40 minutes. Start Final at 10.05 pm
Would like total of 15 for final. No jump-off. Centre of
Arena will be cleared of fences. Tractors used. Band will play.
Red Coats will form up, lining sides to quarter markers.
Awards enter. Cup taken out. Awards will form up facing
Royal Box. Winner out in front. Spots on. Cup will be
presented by Field Marshal Sir Geoffrey Baker. Awards out.
Winner Lap of Honour. Band will play out. Complete with
awards 10.35 pm Mr D. WILLIAMS will announce close of
evening performance. National Anthem.

NOTE: BBC TV 9.25–10.00 and 10.45–11.00 approx.

You will surely agree from the foregoing that there must be one
person who has complete control during a performance. It would truly
be chaos otherwise. But that won't prevent him from handing over to

an assistant for a while, because the instructions have been issued and all thoroughly discussed. That is the value of the conference. In the last chapter I outlined exactly how 'Control' works at the Wembley Pool: the system is I think nearly foolproof provided everyone is on the alert.

The organization in the Collecting Ring is of the greatest importance, for unless there's a steady flow of horses into the arena your show cannot run on time. There should always be an 'outside collecting ring'. The steward in charge calls over the loud speaker to the 'outside' that Number . . . is required, and then Number . . . has a last practise jump before moving to the 'inside' ring: there to wait his turn, usually two to go. If at all unsure, he can have a last look at the Plan of the Course.

If you were standing near 'Control' one night, you might overhear a conversation like the following:—

'Chris, how many more to go?'

'Only one clear, so we have a winner'

'David, how many equal seconds?'

'Four equal second; then we have three equal sixth, and five equal below these . . .'

The Director will then say, 'I only want down to equal sixth for the awards, others will collect rosettes from the Secretary's office.'

'One more to jump.'

'Award stewards, check on rosettes seconds and sixths.'

(To the collecting ring) 'Warn tractors start up, centre to be cleared before awards enter.'

'Raymond, warn band a snatch will be required while centre fences are being cleared.'

And so the show goes on, thanks to that perfectly trained team of stewards, as in the case of any good regiment.

A more, or less, pleasant moment comes in the late afternoon or evening when Major George Worboys, the Show secretary, arrives, with Mr Ron Adams and Mr David Price-Smith, who are in charge of the box office, to discuss the sale of tickets at that particular performance. If the figures are good it will call for a large whisky and soda; if bad or disappointing it will equally call for that whisky and soda while we wring the neck of the question W H Y?

No show, regardless of size, whether outdoor or indoor, can ever succeed unless everyone concerned knows precisely what he or she is expected to do. It won't 'take off' unless all—course builders, caterers, electricians, cleaners, musicians, stewards, judges, directors—all are welded into a perfect team, each madly enthusiastic and longing to make that show a success.

CHAPTER XII

Obstacles and Fences

The success or failure of a jumping competition will depend much on the obstacles and course. A well planned course with well built fences should be interesting to the rider, give encouragement to the best type and trained horse. Further, it should provide pleasure and excitement to the spectator.

Obviously courses for the young or inexperienced horse must be easy; however, in important open competitions the course and obstacles must be testing. There is nothing more dull than to see one out of every two horses jump without fault. The fences then have to be raised and, should there be only one jump-off, considerably so. Time being the deciding factor, the competition develops into a race or speed class over high fences. This is not good for horses, and there is little doubt that the jumping life of a horse is not now as long as it used to be. The pulling of horses round at very sharp turns might be expected in 'speed' or 'time' competitions, but not in open Table A competitions where there will be one or perhaps two jumps-off.

The standard of jumping has so improved in recent years that unless the course builder uses his imagination there will be endless clear rounds. Certainly, the spectator does not wish to see 'trappy' fences or bricks and poles flying in every direction. In a major competition, should there be two jumps-off out of a class of about thirty competitors; the course builder should hope for one in five, that is to say five or six, without faults, and then perhaps two for the second or final jump-off.

Fences should certainly be well built and of solid appearance but now there is a tendency to make them too easy and lacking in imagination. The other factor of great importance is the distances between fences, and here there is a tendency to make every distance absolutely correct. This, of course, does not give any advantage to the well trained and obedient horse. Therefore I believe distances should not always be correct. These two major factors will be dealt with later.

When discussing jumps, a fence is one that requires one effort of the horse; an obstacle is when two or three fences are so placed that the distance between the inside elements of each fence does not exceed 39 ft 4 in (12 m). Should the distance be any more, then they are single fences.

An obstacle should be numbered as one. Thus, should a treble be the third on the course it would be 3A, 3B and 3C.

There are three main types of fences: the 'straight' fence has a completely vertical face such as a gate or wall; the 'spread' fence requires the horse to spread himself as well as possibly jumping high and this will have a vertical face; the third type is the 'staircase' fence which again requires the horse to spread himself, but it is made easier for him since the fence is built on a slope—the most common, of course, being the triple bar.

The horse, when approaching a fence, will or should have lowered his head and will be judging the point at which to take off from the bottom of the fence or what is termed the 'groundline'.

Groundlines play a very important part in the building of a fence. The horse will normally take off in a zone of between the height and the height and a half of the fence. That is to say, should the fence be a 4 ft (1.2 m) high gate, the horse should take off in a zone of 4 ft to 6 ft (1.8 m) from the base of the fence. Should there be no groundline, as in the case of a single pole, the fence becomes more difficult. Should there be a wall or brush placed behind a single rail, the fence becomes still more difficult and this is known as a false groundline: the tendency will be for the horse to take off too close to the fence, having judged the take off point from the base of the brush standing behind the rail.

Undoubtedly there is a growing tendency to provide every fence with a perfect groundline. This is probably correct when building for young horses but in major competitions it removes the advantage from the well trained and obedient horse. Post and rails, gates, vertical walls and naturally straight fences should not, save in exceptional cases, be provided with artificial groundlines, such as shrubs.

Shadows often provide good natural groundlines. For example, a large gate, so placed that the horse is jumping into the sun, will become so much the easier with the shadow on the take off side. Should it be wished to encourage the horses to stand back, the wings or shrubs may be pulled towards the take off side. Groundlines will be dealt with later in greater detail as the building of individual fences is discussed.

Fences should normally be either 12 ft (3.7 m) as used at the smaller shows or 15 ft (4.5 m) in width. If 12 ft the elements such as brush or walls should be built in sections of 5 ft 10 in (1.8 m), if 15 ft then in sections of 4 ft 10 in or 7 ft 4 in (1.4 or 2.2 m) The wider the fence the easier it is to jump. This because, should the horse be coming at a wrong take off distance, the rider may jump the fence at an angle, unless it be a large spread fence.

'A' 1"x1/4" Half Round Section

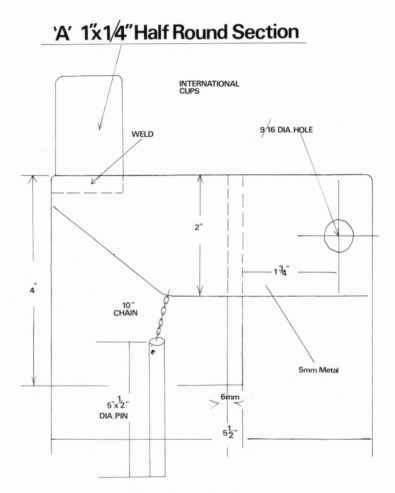

Fig. a. International Cup.

Poles should be round, 4 in (10 cm) in diameter. The fittings should be of uniform size and under international rules the pole must not be more than half its diameter in the cup. That is to say, in the case of 4 in diameter the cup should not be more than 2 in (5 cm) deep (see diagram).

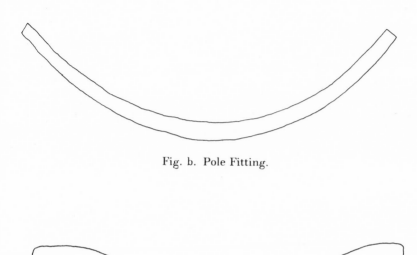

Fig. b. Pole Fitting.

Fig. c. International Fitting for Gate or Plank.

Poles are best made of larch and a 12 ft pole when new will weigh about 35 lbs (15.8 kg) whereas a 15 ft pole will weigh about 45 lbs (20.4 kg).

The fitting for gates and heavy planks must always be almost flat and a mark on the fittings should be cut to ensure the gate or plank is always replaced in the same position (see diagram). Should rustic poles be used (often silver birch of irregular shape), the course builder must mark the top pole and have a similar one ready should this pole be broken.

The brush fence is intended to represent a hedge and is usually made by packing a wooden frame with birch, which is then trimmed to the required height and shape. Scots fir or deal is most suitable for the frame. The frame should be either 4 ft 10 in (1.47 m) or 5 ft 10 in (1.77 m) long., 2 ft 6 in (.76 m) high and 1 ft (.30 m) deep. The feet should be similar to those used for stands but smaller. Elm or hemlock may be used if necessary for the feet, as it is heavy. Fences should not be packed too tight on account of weight. Green birch should be used. The brush should not be clipped so that it bulges towards the take off, this is unnatural.

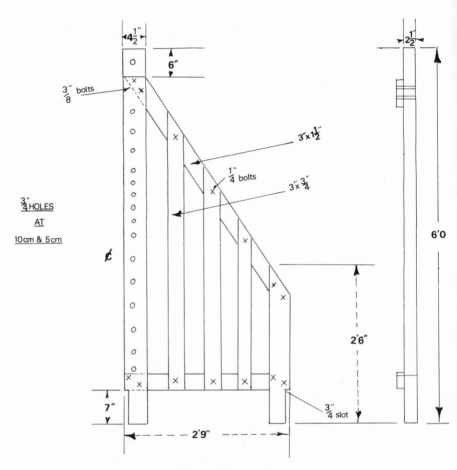

Fig. d. Wing Stand.

The stands or uprights which carry the elements' poles must always be strong and heavy at the feet. They should be 4 in by 4 in (10 cm by 10 cm), of a standard size in order that the fittings may be changed. In height they should average from 3 ft (.9 m) to 6 ft (1.8 m). The majority should be from 4 ft 6 in (1.4 m) to 5 ft 3 in (1.6 m). Stands may be constructed with the wings or be a single post with a heavy foot (see diagram). Undoubtedly the most suitable wood is oak; it certainly is heavy but once built the fence is firm. The posts should be drilled at 2 in (5 cm) intervals to suit the universal fitting. To prevent these holes from shrinking in wet weather it is advisable to run a hot iron through each hole. Larch may be used but it is liable to split at the pin holes.

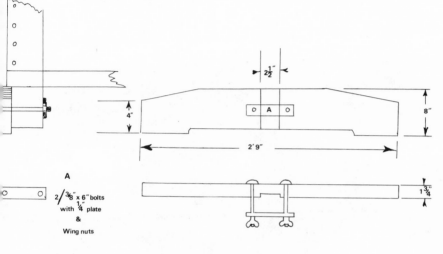

Fig. e. Detachable Feet.

The most important part of the stand is the foot which must be heavy to stand firm in a gale. The foot of the stand may be made of elm or hemlock. Feet should be detachable in order to facilitate transport. It may, at times, in gales, be necessary to peg the feet.

A *single rail* is a natural obstacle but having no groundline is the more difficult to jump. To make it easier, a red lamp, as for a road closed, could be placed directly under the pole. Single poles should not be over 4 ft 3 in (1.3 m) or possibly 4 ft 6 in (1.4 m) in height. When used as doubles or even trebles, they are difficult, but attractive to the spectator.

Perhaps the most common use of rails or poles is as a natural post and rails. This is a *straight fence*. Should the poles be taken right down to nearly ground level, the fence becomes less natural but is easier to jump.

[81]

The *triple bar* is perhaps the most common of staircase fences. It is good to watch and very easy for the horse. The staircase fence can be ridden at with confidence. The bottom rail should be about 18 in (45 cm) from the ground. Rather than have all the rails equally spaced, to help the horse it is better to have the second rail slightly higher. If the fence is large, the centre rail must be high as this encourages the horse to bascule in the best style.

The *hog's back* is a very simple fence. It is merely a post and rails with a rail on either side: a good fence for a young horse.

23. Wilf White, G.B., on Nizefela.

24. Christian Rey, Switzerland, a young rider jumping the magnificent
heather bank at Lucerne.

Parallel bars: this in reality is two post and rails fences built parallel
and is difficult. The take off is straight, yet the horse is required to
spread, so must take off at the correct place. If the front pole is lower
than the second the fence becomes easier, being almost a staircase
fence. If the rails stand at 4 ft 6 in with a 5 ft (1.5 m) spread the
obstacle is extremely testing.

The *double oxer* represents the natural cut and laid hedge with an
ox rail on either side. According to how it is built, it can be a difficult
or easy obstacle. Should it be built with a single rail standing about 3 ft
(.9 m) and well away on the take off side it has a false groundline.
Should there be two or three rails on the take off side the obstacle then
becomes easier. Only one rail should ever be used on the landing side,
to avoid an accident.

A *reversed oxer*, as its name implies is the opposite to the double
oxer and it should represent two hedges and a rail in the centre; it is an

[83]

easy fence and as such can be placed as an early spread in any course.

The *gate* is a natural fence, typical in British show jumping courses. It is a pure straight fence. It should be made of oak or larch and at least 12 ft (3.7 m) wide. The top and bottom rails should be of 5 in (12.5 cm) by 3 in (7.5 cm). If, when raised so that the bottom rail is more than 6 in (15 cm) off the ground, a pole of the same colour should be placed directly underneath. There are many types of fancy gates. Some picked out in colours or with red discs as for railway crossings. Perhaps the best variations are those made with a concave or convex top rail. Should the gate be liable to swing, it should be pegged at the foot. Gates should be built without diagonal cross braces for fear that the horse may catch his foot in these and injure the fetlock joint.

Walls are natural fences in any country and in some permanent arenas there are solid stone walls standing about 4 ft (1.2 m); above these solid walls poles may be used. Although artificial walls are difficult and cumbersome to move, they should always be included in courses. The wall is an excellent straight fence and it is usually well jumped. The colour and height will depend upon what the wall is intended to represent: it may be grey stone, red brick or concrete but when painted should look natural and be an added attraction in the arena. The wall must be constructed in sections of either 5 ft 10 in (1.77 m) or for a 15 ft (4.57 m) wall, 4 ft 10 in (1.47 m) sections. Elm is the most suitable material for the 'bricks' and the weight of the bricks 18 in by 9 in by 3 in (45 by 22.8 by 7.5 cm) would be 10 lbs (4.5 kg): 24 in by 9 in by 3 in (61 by 22.8 by 7.5 cm) would weigh 13 lbs (5.9 kg). The top blocks, 12 in by 10 in by 3 in (30.4 by 25.4 by 7.5 cm) would weigh 7 lbs (3.1 kg).

The wall may be built straight on one side with a slight slope on the other and so, according to the direction in which it is jumped, may be easier or more difficult. The wall may be varied by placing a single rail some 2 ft (.6 m) or more on the landing side. The top of the wall should be rounded and might even have a parapet or layer of tiles. In both cases this will provide an overlap of 2 in or 4 in (5 or 10 cm) making the obstacle just that much more difficult.

A water jump is essential to any major outdoor course, however it is not necessary in an indoor arena. In certain competitions such as the Nations Cup where a water jump is obligatory (except indoors), poles may not be used over the water; however in other competitions they may, and they certainly make the jumping of this fence easier. A small brush fence of 2 ft in height, or a similar element, should be used on the take off side and this must be fixed.

It is advisable to build a permanent water jump which can be jumped in either direction. The actual spread of the water should be

25. Fritz Ligges, Germany, on Genius—he was a member of the victorious German team at the 1972 Olympics in Munich.

12 ft (3.7 m). The soil should be dug out with a centre depth of 12 in to 18 in (30 to 45 cm) afterwards lining the depression with concrete or puddling with clay. From the centre it will shelve up to a depth of 2 in or 3 in (5 or 7.5 cm). If concrete is used it must be lined with

[85]

either rubber or coconut mats to prevent the horse slipping. The face
of the approach should never be less than 14 ft (4.3 m) wide, and never
must the width of the approach be less than the length of the water.
The wider the approach, the easier the water is to jump.

The landing edge of the water must be marked by a white strip of
plasticine just in the water. This plasticine will be spread in a narrow
tray of 3 in (7.5 cm) in width.

To encourage novice horses to jump water a rail should be placed
over it or, perhaps even better, a small post and rails placed as a fence
29 ft (8.8 m) in front of the water, thus making it a combination (or
one obstacle) which will ensure that the horse takes off close to the
fence, and so clears the water with ease.

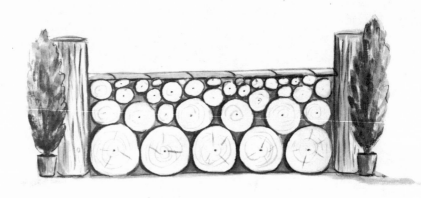

xvii   If the imagination is used the variety becomes almost end-

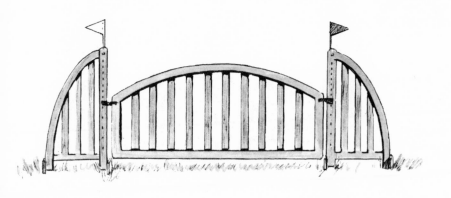

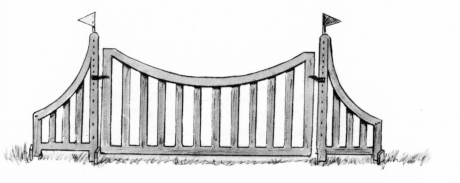

less. To the course builder the fences must be his scenery.

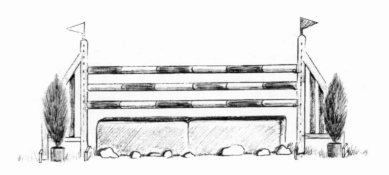

xviii. More imagination will create greater interest

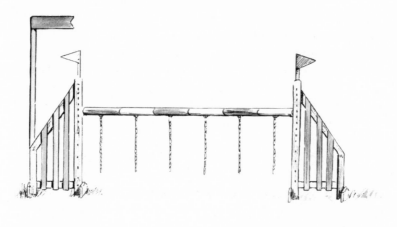

nd colour for the rider and the spectator.

Narrow fences such as stiles require obedience. A stile should be 6 ft (1.8 m) in width on the approach and if placed towards the end of a course requires concentration by the rider. The step of the stile provides a good groundline. In a combination, there is no reason why a stile should not be placed as the second fence and this to one side, in order that the rider jumps in over a formidable fence, and then either follows straight on over another large fence or swings right or left over the smaller stile.

The stile may be substituted by a wicket gate, which is slightly more difficult, being an absolutely straight fence. The same principles apply to walls where, should the wall be part of the combination, the second part might be lower or a broken wall slightly to one side.

Fences built in curved form demand concentration and obedience. If approached on the outside of the curve the fence is simple, for the horse is encouraged to take off early by the curve. If against the curve, it is very much more difficult.

The course builder, when driving through the countryside, must always be on the lookout for new ideas. His object must be to try to give the advantage to the best jumper which has been well trained and is obedient, and not to build a course that, lacking in imagination, gives the advantage to a horse which has great power but is not so thoroughly trained.

If the imagination is used the variety becomes almost endless: concave and convex gates, stiles and narrow wicket· gates demanding obedience during the approach, railway crossings with staring red discs and continental railway crossings involving single pole with hanging chains. The Canadian snake fence made of rustic material is not only attractive but provides one more test of obedience, for the fence must be jumped at an angle.

In the case of a stile being placed in the centre, or in an outside portion of a wall, this also demands complete obedience.

Finally flags must mark the extremities of all fences, red on the right and white on the left. Under international rules these may be fixed to the fence. Fences must be numbered and it is advisable to have two sets of numbers, each set a different colour.

CHAPTER XIII

The Influence of Distances between Fences

Before the Second World War the rider did not seriously consider the distances between individual fences, and although he assessed the distances in combinations or obstacles, these did not influence his riding to the extent they do now. In the hunting field, jumping in and out of a lane, the rider corrected his stride by instinct. We did not study or pace distances between individual fences. However in my 'Trick Ride', when jumping small walls or swords stuck in the ground, we had the distances carefully measured. For example if jumping a line of sixteen narrow walls without bridles and no non-jumping stride in between, the distances would be 9 ft 6 in (2.9 m) for the first eight or so and then gradually decreased to 9 ft (2.7 m) as the bridleless horse lost impetus. For the swords standing at about 3 ft 3 in (.98 m) with one non-jumping stride we would allow 17 ft or 18 ft (5.2 m or 5.5 m).

However, since those days the art of show jumping has so improved that nothing can be left to chance and the rider will carefully measure the distances between individual fences, possibly up to a distance of 82 ft (25 m).

Now, a result in a major competition can only be achieved if heights of fences are raised excessively and then jumped at great speed. The competition develops into a race over high obstacles or fences and this is not good for horses: therefore experienced course builders should provide problems of distances. If in a line of fences the distances are absolutely correct, the rider jumping the first fence in the line properly will find he is 'right' for the remaining fences in that line.

Under international rules the measurement between fences in com-

[91]

26. Harvey Smith, G.B., on O'Malley, over a wall and gate.

binations is taken from the inside element of the first fence to the inside element of the next. This is a formula for course builders and obviously riders will have their own individual methods of measuring.

The average stride of the horse is probably from 11 ft 3 in (3.4 m) to 12 ft (3.7 m) when galloping on at a speed of 383 yards per minute (350 m). But, of course, this will vary with different horses, and the conditions of the ground. If wet and heavy, the length of the stride will be less. If there is ample room between fences and the horse can gallop on, the stride will be longer. Indoors on the other hand, although the going will be perfect, the stride will be shorter.

The horse will take off about the height of the fence and a half away. That is to say, should the fence be 4 ft (1.2 m) high, the horse will take off about 6 ft (1.8 m) away or possibly 5 ft (1.5 m), according to the rider's wishes. The horse will land about 6 ft 6 in (2 m) beyond the fence; thus he lands further than the distance from which he takes off at this straight fence of 4 ft (1.2 m) high. Should the fence be a straight fence of 5 ft 3 in (1.6 m), he will take off at about 6 ft 3 in (1.9 m) away and will land 7 ft 3 in (2.2 m) beyond the fence. Should the fence be 6 ft (1.8 m) in height, he will take off at a distance of about 7 ft (2.1 m remaining in the zone which would be 6 ft to 9 ft (1.8—2.7 m). He will land about 7 ft 6 in (2.3 m) beyond the fence.

From this it is clear that the horse will, in comparison to the height of the fence, land closer as the fence rises, because the higher the fence the more perfect should be the bascule of the horse.

When at the Equitation School, Weedon, we as pupils each day had to do physical training, and one of the most unpleasant exercises was a dive over the high horse. This was to teach us to tuck in our heads in the case of a fall, and the higher the vaulting horse became the more we had to round our backs and do a perfect bascule. Needless to say our PT instructor gave the necessary assistance to ensure we did not hurt ourselves unduly.

An obstacle or combination of fences must not exceed, under the international rules, a distance of 39 ft 4 in (11.98 m). Distances exceeding this between individual fences might be relative to three, four or five strides. They are relative to a stride of 12 ft (3.7 m) or over. Thus, a true three-stride distance between two fences, allowing 6 ft (1.8 m) each for landing and take off is 48 ft (14.6 m). A true four stride distance is 59 ft (18 m); for five strides the distance would be 71 ft (21.6 m) and a six stride would be 82 ft (25 m) which allows the stride to be 11 ft 8 in (3.6 m).

27. Anneli Drummond-Hay, G.B., riding Merely-a-Monarch. This horse was not only supreme in show jumping but also in Three-Day Eventing. Note the contact with perfect hands.

28. Neil Shapiro, U.S.A., riding Trick Track, off a bank and over a pole.
Both very alert.

These distances are between independent fences and the course
builder will possibly set problems in order that the horse which has
been well trained must shorten his stride to take five, or lengthen to
take four strides. This will give the advantage to an obedient horse
which has been well trained on the flat.

These distance problems should only be used by experienced course
builders. When a very free jumping course is set, and if the going is
very good, then up to 3 ft (.9 m) may be added to distances of more
than three strides (i.e. 59 ft + 3 ft (18 + 0.9 m) etc.). For treble
fences, one must be careful not to set one distance short and the other
long (or the other way round which is worse). One should set either
two short distances which have to be ridden steadily, or two long
distances which must be ridden strongly, or a true distance followed
by a long distance where the horse must be ridden strongly after
landing over the first obstacle. The problem of the short distance can

be introduced by reducing the true distance by 1 ft or 18 in (30 cm or 45 cm) and the problem of the long distance by increasing the true distance from 1 ft to 2 ft (30 cm to 60 cm). If these limits are exceeded it is likely that one will present horses and riders with an insoluble problem, as was the case in the Olympic Games in 1960 when the individual competition had a treble of almost impossible distances.

When varying distances from true, this does tend to give some horses an advantage: those who are obedient and well trained will definitely have the advantage in a jump-off against the clock.

For combination obstacles, the following are considered to be true distances for the average horse in an open competition, according to the type of obstacle or combination:—

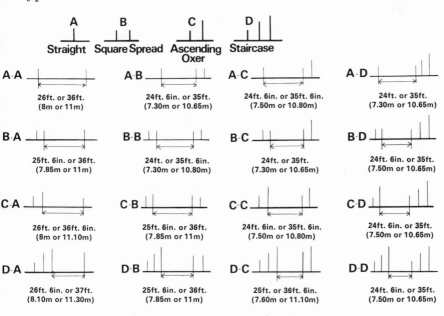

Fig. f. Distances between combinations.

CHAPTER XIV

Designing the Course

Having dealt in detail in the two previous chapters with the building of fences and the problems of distances, between them, it is now time to discuss the planning of the complete course.

The president, or senior member of the judge's panel or jury, is responsible for checking the course and obstacles: however, should the course builder be an experienced person it is usually left to him, although the judge, when walking around, may make certain minor adjustments in heights and spreads.

With the equipment of well made obstacles and fences, carefully planned courses will provide jumping of a high standard giving encouragement to the horses and pleasure to the riders and the spectators. Above all the course builder must be an enthusiast who has the necessary knowledge and experience of the work.

To plan a good course requires much time and it cannot be done on the day of the show in a hurry. The true course builder will derive as much pride and pleasure from his finished production as any great artist.

Whether it be a small one day show or a major international one, either indoors or out, the course builder must plan in advance. To do this he must know the size of the arena, the conditions of the classes in the programme and what material he will have available.

In the early days of the Royal International Horse Show, and at the birth of the Horse of the Year Show in 1949, when I was not only directing the show but planning and checking the courses, I was fool enough to think I could do it more or less on the spot. This does not work. Apart from planning the course for one particular competition.

[96]

29. Colonel E. A. Haccius,
Switzerland, the greatest architect
of show jumping courses.

Planning a show jumping
se with my special magnetic
l.

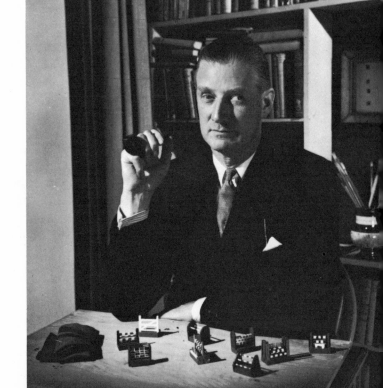

the builder must be thinking of the next. Is it necessary to move every fence? Cannot the fence be changed in character and so avoid having to move a heavy wall or brush? The answer to all these questions can only be decided at home and prior to the show.

An outside arena should have a good springy turf. Should the going be hard it will be necessary to water the landings or ease the turf with a fork. If the going is likely to become slippery through rain, there should be an ample supply of coarse sand.

The going is of the utmost importance and well do I remember having a flood at the White City during the Royal International Horse Show. At 7.00 pm the arena was under water. No tractor carrying sand could leave the outside cinder track. Nevertheless, with the help of the magnificent arena party from the Household Cavalry, sharp grit was wheeled in, barrowful after barrowful, and then that night we had the most superb jumping.

Many may be the problems of the indoor show but with the floor at the Empire Pool, Wembley, we have, I believe, the best in the world. The floor is laid over the old swimming pool. Over this the pipes, laid in sand, are ready to freeze the floor for the ice and, in actual fact, on occasions our floor has been laid on the ice. First the boards, covered with paper in order to keep them clean; on top of the boards, 4 inches (10 cm) of very tightly packed loam; then the mixture of one part sieved loam, one part sand and one part sawdust. The mixture is laid to a depth of 2 inches (5 cm) and a good covering of salt to keep the top moist.

Courses should not, other than in exceptional cases, be too long: from 700 yds (640 m) to 800 yds (731.5 m) is admirable. As television plays a great part in our sport today, it is important that there should be no long distances between fences. Nothing can be more dull for the spectator, or television viewer, than to watch a horse hit the second or third fence and then, although out of the running for the competition, continuing with what we might call a tedious round, tedious for everybody.

Indoors, an ideal arena should be 80 yds (73.2 m) long by 40 yds (36.6 m).

In the outdoor arena it is better to build the course in the centre, allowing a track of some 10 yds (9.2 m) around the outside. This will allow for the judging of hunter, hacks and harness classes.

Knowing the size of the arena the course builder must now carefully study the programme and the conditions of each competition. The following principles should be observed:

a. Use as many fences as possible within reason. An ordinary course should have at least 9 or 10 fences.

b. The course must always, if possible, have two or three or even more changes of direction.

c. Straight and spread fences should be varied.

d. At least one combination or obstacle should be provided, if possible two or three.

e. The course should begin with at least three easy fences, so that the horse and rider gain confidence.

f. Difficult fences, such as large spreads, should never be placed near the collecting ring. It is easier to jump towards the collecting ring than away from it.

g. The spectacular fences must be well placed for the spectators. Remember that there are spectators all around the arena, and not only in the expensive seats.

h. Should the same fence have to be jumped twice, sufficient time must be allowed to rebuild it if it is knocked down. It should be an easy fence to rebuild, such as a gate.

The course builder, having studied the programme and conditions and the size of the arena, now drafts a plan of the course with the track and fences. He does not at this stage consider detail as to the make up of each fence. Nevertheless he should decide which are to be spreads, straight or staircase fences (see diagram for Table 'A' course out of doors) and naturally, where the combinations are to be placed.

When planning, the course builder will vary the fences, allowing for the simple, or inviting ones, at the early part of the course. Gradually he will build up the fences and the difficulties, to create excitement towards the end of the course.

Every fence must be planned with a definite object: the first three or four to give encouragement to the horse and rider, followed by the test fences. The wide spread followed possibly by a large straight fence or, on the other hand, perhaps two large spread fences to get the horse galloping on, quickly followed by a straight fence to test obedience. Then the combination to test obedience and suppleness, and the small gate or stile for complete obedience; often if such a fence is placed towards the end of the course, and particularly after large fences, the rider will lose his concentration, (like many a great cricketer approaching his century,) and down will come this small fence placed for that very purpose.

[99]

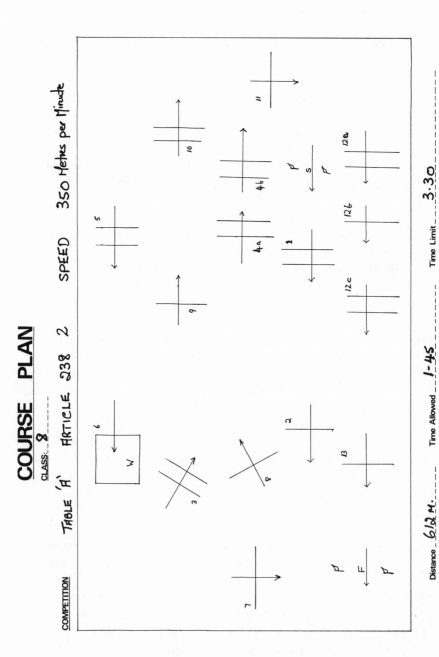

Fig. g. Plan of Table A course for an outdoor arena as posted on notice board.

The first and second fences should be firmly fixed and then if the horse takes a liberty he may get away with no fault and will jump better during the remainder of the round. Often, in fact almost regularly, I have been standing listening intently during a round, and so hoping one of the British horses would win that I have been relieved to hear after a good hard knock that no part of the fence falls. It is that little bit of luck that wins.

In every major competition a water jump should be included and this should not, as in past years, always be the last fence. Out hunting the brook may be met during any part of the hunt, so this should be the case in a show jumping course.

It is wrong to place a fence at the end or across the entrance and exit.

It is impossible for the course builder, when designing his courses prior to the show, to decide on the size of the fence, as the actual size on the day will depend upon a variety of circumstances as listed below. There are factors applicable to all courses.

First, whatever the competition, one competitor *should* jump the course without fault. I well remember Colonel Haccius emphazising this to me. If no horse jumps a clear round, the course is not a good one. Secondly, except for the first three or so fences, the faults should be evenly distributed; there should not be any 'bogey' fences or traps.

The course builder will therefore decide how many clear rounds he hopes can be ridden for an important competition: it is the same as paying the same wage to the unskilled worker as to the skilled; a mediocre horse, if the luck is with him, is just as likely to jump a clear round over a small course as a really top class horse.

At small shows and in novice competitions, the courses should be set for the average competitor. These small shows are the nursery of show jumping and everything should be done to encourage the rider and the young horse. This may mean a large number of clear rounds: then the course may be raised and at times considerably, except in novice classes. In a competition confined to these latter, fences should never be unduly raised: it can mean disaster to a young horse who perhaps may lose his nerve and never compete again with success.

As I have already stated, in jumping competitions there are always certain rules and conditions and the course builder must carefully study these when preparing his plans. He will not decide on heights until he knows the standard of the horses for which he has to set the course; he must also take into consideration the conditions of the arena

[101]

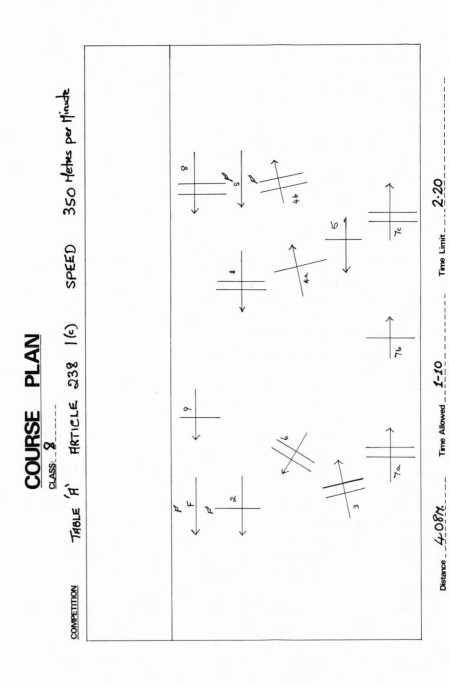

Fig. h. Plan of Table A course for an indoor arena as posted on notice board.

and the materials at his disposal. However, there are certain considerations if not rules, he should remember:

a. The condition of the going. If heavy or slippery quite obviously the heights must be reduced.

b. The position of the fence in the course. If early it must be smaller until the horse and rider have got their blood up. A fence, coming towards the collecting ring, will be jumped more readily than if turning away from the collecting ring or exit.

c. The site of the fence. If it is placed after a sharp turn with only a short approach, as is often the case with an indoor arena, or if the ground is not level (particularly downhill or when the background makes the fence difficult to see) the fence should be smaller.

d. The nature of the fence and the material with which it is built. A well made fence, attractive to jump, may be built larger than a more difficult one which may not necessarily be flimsy but may have no groundline or even a false groundline.

In a championship or major competition, if out of doors there should always be a minimum of twelve fences, and these should include two combinations making a total of at least fourteen to fifteen efforts. Among them there should be a water jump. In an indoor arena the number of fences should be reduced to nine, with one or two combinations, making a minimum total of eleven efforts. Whether out or in, there must be at least two changes of direction.

The Puissance is a competition designed to test the capability and power of the horse to jump large obstacles or fences. The fences in the Puissance course should be divided equally between spreads and straight fences. The size of the obstacles should be progressively increased in spread and height. In the first round, the size of the fences should be set so that at least a third of the horses competing will be without fault.

In recent years the inclination has been to reduce the course in the second and third rounds to a minimum of two fences and then increase the height of the second or straight fence to achieve some such record as 7 ft 4 in (2.2 m). This practice may at times succeed but after years of experience I am convinced it is wrong. The horse is made to continue jumping until he either refuses or fails. I now believe that the fences in jump-off courses should never be reduced in number to less than four or five and, with the exception of the first fence, all the rest should be raised or widened. Then the competition will not become a high jump.

In competitions designed for speed the fences should never be high, for these competitions are a test not only of jumping but obedience. This applies to 'Touch and Out', 'Relay' and 'Take you own Line' competitions.

In these speed competitions the course should be so designed that there is the opportunity for the rider to take a shorter course by, perhaps, cutting inside another fence.

Every show and arena will be different. It would be a sad day if shows, great or small, became exactly the same. It is important that each should maintain its own individual personality.

If possible, the course builder should know what material he will have available to build his fences and ask for extra material such as

31. The picturesque arena at Lucerne with the lake in the background.

bales of straw, shrubs or bundles of peasticks to provide filling.

Most important of all he should arrive at the show with the plans of the courses ready drawn.

The plan need only give the position and the nature of the fences. The start and finish should be clearly indicated, each fence shown by a single line if a straight fence, or by a double line if a spread or staircase. Each fence or obstacle should be numbered. Unless it is necessary for the riders to take a particular track, it should not be marked with a continuous line; turning flags should also be avoided unless absolutely necessary.

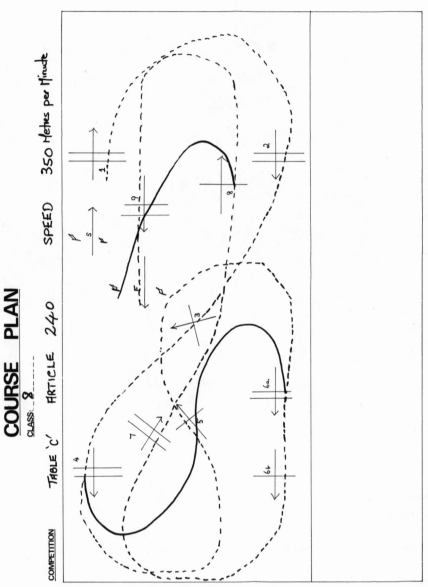

Fig. i. Plan of Table C course. The dotted line shows the measured track. The continuous line shows where a rider, by taking risks, might gain time.

I only intend to deal with the duties at a major show, running over two or three days or even a week. The principles are nevertheless the same for the smaller, although no less important, one day show.

The 'tempo' of a show must be maintained and it is certainly more difficult to do this indoors. It can with all honesty be said that the organization and production of the major shows in Britain are a long way in advance of those in other countries: consequently our shows pay their way.

If this building of courses or changing of the scenery is to be carried out efficiently, the builder must have the opportunity to carry out a reconnaissance or rehearsal on the day before the opening.

He will then check his fences and all his material. He should start by building the course for the major competition on the first day. He will carefully measure distances, and mark the position of the stands for the fences on the ground. This should be done with paint or whitewash.

The course builder will then practice changing this course to the next, again marking with paint the position of fences. Where fences are on a diagonal, it is advisable to use a large set square to ensure these fences are in correct line, also always to lay down a line and carefully use a measuring tape.

In an indoor arena it is not possible to mark the position with whitewash or paint the floor, so marks may be made on the wall or on diagonals laid on a string which has coloured markings, to indicate the position of those fences on the diagonals. In an outdoor arena it's probable that the courses for the first day will be built beforehand.

When the lay-out is marked, the track must be measured with a wheel, generously; it should be that of a careful rider taking no short cuts. Should a measuring wheel not be available, use a measuring tape or pace it out. If the latter, two should definitely do it independently. At the same time measure the track for the jump-off.

The next duty of the course builder will be to set the heights and spreads (these are not marked on the plan). When doing this, he will take account of the following:—

a. The conditions of the competition.

b. The number of horses who have declared to compete.

c. The standard of these horses.

When finally adjusting the fences, he will make notes as to the heights and spreads and, if necessary, mark with chalk on the stands the position of each pole or element. Should a fence be completely

[107]

knocked down it is absolutely essential that it be erected as it was for the previous competitors. Unless these written notes are made, and if necessary the stands marked, mistakes can easily occur.

The position of shrubs or wings must be carefully studied and noted.

Lastly, the course builder must see that there is sufficient material to replace broken poles or even gates. He should then check the plan of the course and that of the jump-off.

On the plan must be the distance of the course, time allowed, and the time limit which is always twice the time allowed (see course plans). There should be no indication of distances between fences. Should the course for the jump-off be very different, it may be advisable to have a separate plan for this.

Once the competition has started the plan of the course must never be altered. The course builder must have one, and also the judges and the commentator. These three plans should also show the distances and heights.

Before the competitors are permitted to walk the course, the senior judge should have checked that it is set in accordance with the plan and conditions of the competition.

When the competition is in progress, the course builder or his

32. Caroline Bradley, G.B., on Franco, jumping parallels over water in the beautiful Piazza da Siena in Rome.

33. Alison Westwood, G.B., with The Maverick over a bank and rail.

assistant will always be in the arena. Fences knocked down should not be rebuilt until the competitor has completed his round, except in the case of a refusal.

Should a fence be completely demolished, the senior course builder must supervise the rebuilding, measuring and checking with his notes that it is rebuilt with exactly the same spread and height.

The judges should never give the signal to start until the course builder has given his signal that all is ready.

As the competition progresses the course builder will be carefully considering the course for a jump-off and what fences will have to be enlarged or raised. And if it is an indoor show, he will be planning what fences will be removed for the presentation at the completion of the competition.

The course builder is a very important official. He has unlimited duties to carry out and much of the success or failure of the show depends upon him. He must know his facts, have complete confidence in himself and endlessly use his imagination.

CHAPTER XV

The Spectator

As I have tried to make clear throughout this Guide to Show Jumping, while excellence of horse, rider and course are of primary importance, the spectator also plays an essential part in a successful show and should receive constant consideration in all planning of events.

One of the greatest joys of show jumping for the spectator is that the rules are so simple to understand. There are really no matters of opinion and so no equivalent of 'Was Bill Smith offside? . . . No, ref you're WRONG . . . Was that a foot fault? . . . Was the ball on the line? . . . Why did the chalk fly then? etc. etc.'

Anyone in the stand or by the ringside can quickly learn the rules and judge for himself. Here I shall be explaining the international rules although there's now little difference between them and those of the British Show Jumping Association.

Let's imagine that my friend Jack and his family are sitting with me in the stands. Jack says he knows little about it, so I'll explain. As we sit and gaze down at the brilliant arena, riders are walking around the course, some by themselves, others in groups. As we know, in international competitions they are allowed to walk the course in this way, for they must not only memorise the track, or way round, and the order in which fences are jumped, but they might also wish to pace the distances between individual fences, particularly in combinations; with these latter a fence will be numbered, say, 9A, followed by 9B and possibly 9C.

We've already explained that the average stride of a horse will be about 11 ft 6 in (3.5 m). A rider knows that to arrive at the correct take off point he may either have to shorten or lengthen his horse's stride. That's why he'll be carefully checking the distances down there, and studying the make up of each fence.

Jack is naturally interested to see the well known champions, the Harvey Smiths, the David Broomes, but is also intrigued to notice Debbie Johnsey, the European Junior Individual Champion 1973, who is only seventeen, and Tony Newbery of Devonshire who represented Great Britain at Aachen when only twenty. Here too comes Graham Fletcher, now a veteran of twenty-four who with Derek Ricketts helped us to win the Nations Cup in New York for the first time ever, in 1973. I explained to Jack how lucky it had been that we'd thought well ahead, and encouraged young riders to compete abroad. For we now have a tremendous reserve of international riders, more so probably than any other country.

There goes a touch on the bell, signal for riders to leave the ring. Those who have drawn early will have to look sharp to warm up. Obviously the draw is of considerable importance if you're competing: you can then watch, if you're drawn late, how one or two of your friends cope with the problems awaiting you.

I quickly explain to Jack about our having three or four judges, and, as there are riders from several countries, one of these must be

34. Pierre Jonquères d'Oriola, France, riding Voulette and jumping a pallisade gate at Nice in 1954. D'Oriola is the only rider to have won two Individual Gold Medals at the Olympics in 1952 and 1964.

foreign. They're sitting just up behind us, together with the Time Keeper. I explain also that timing is recorded automatically: the moment a horse goes through the start an electronic ray is broken and the clock records, to 1/10th of a second, until the rider passes through another electronic ray and the clock stops; almost simultaneously another machine near the judges stamps the time on a card; one of the three writes the number of the horse on this card; finally, as a precaution, they have three stop watches just in case something goes wrong with the automatic clock.

Looking at the programme, Jack remarks that there seems to be an awfully large number of entries—Shall we be here all night? I explain how, in most classes, although a rider may have entered two or three horses he can in fact ride one only. In the Grand Prix under international rules that is invariably so, otherwise the 'pluralist' would have an advantage.

At an important show the rider, or horse owner, will have declared his choice that morning, probably before 10 am. The organizer thus knows the number of starters.

Jack wonders whether the style of a rider matters? To which I reply, 'No, there are no marks for style. There are two main types of competition: those you see in your programme marked Table A are a real test of jumping, over high and wide fences at not too fast a pace. Those under Table B or C are over smaller fences, with more turns or changes of direction, and the horse must be very obedient for time has great influence; therefore if he can turn quickly and jump at speed he will have the advantage.'

We now take a look down at the various fences. Some straight like that gate and those two lots of post and rails i.e. they have a vertical face. Then there are the ones which require a horse to spread himself as well as conquer the height: that double oxer there, at number 4. Those two marked 6A and 6B are a combination, a double in this case: since they're not more than 39 ft 4 in apart (12 m), they must be jumped as one obstacle; that is to say, if he refuses at 6B he must come back and jump the first part 6A again before going on. Farther over there you can see what we call a treble, three fences marked 9A, 9B and 9C. As in the double all three must be jumped as one: even if he only refuses at the third, he must go back and rejump the other two.

Well now, this is a Table A competition and should part of a fence be knocked down or dislodged it means 4 penalty points. There are two exceptions to this: if it falls after you've passed through the finish, that doesn't count; and if an element in the same vertical plane *other* than the top element is dislodged, leaving the top one intact, that doesn't count either.

'What about that lovely blue water?' asks Jack.

'You see that white strip on the landing side?' I reply. 'It's made of plasticine, and if a horse lands with any foot on it, or any foot in the water, that's 4 faults. However, if that small fence at the 'take off' is broken or knocked down, there's no penalty.'

'Here comes the first horse!'

The rider salutes the judges and moves about the arena, but he's careful not to go near a fence, for he will be eliminated if he shows his horse any of these before starting.

'Surely it's an advantage not to go early?' Jack says. 'How do they decide on the order? Obviously some will watch these earlier ones?'

'The order's drawn well before the beginning of the show, and for each competition it's rotated. If a hundred horses compete, and there are ten competitions, after the first, the bottom ten are moved to the top of the draw, and so on in order.'

The bell sounds, and the rider is still cantering quietly about the ring, letting his horse get the feel of the atmosphere. I explain that some riders halt and rein their horses back to get them obedient, but in any case they must start within a minute of the bell or be eliminated.

35. Ann Moore, G.B., on Psalm, Ladies European Champion and Olympic Individual Silver Medallist in 1972.

Now he's through the start, and the big digit clock ticks away. Over the first with ease, the second and third, now to number 6, that double.

'You saw there he took two strides between fences, but the first after landing looked short and obviously the rider checked him. I expect the distance has been set as a problem, and is a bit short for two non jumping strides.'

A rail's fallen at that post and rails—but no fault; it's an under rail and the top one's intact in the same vertical plane.

Ah, but there's a top brick on the ground from that wall—4 faults it must be!

The judge by the water has raised his flag—either he went in or landed on the tape—another 4 faults. With a water jump it's nearly always necessary to have a judge in the ring, otherwise there's nobody there but the course builder, and that arena party at the sides, ready to attend to fences when the rider has completed.

The last fence clear, and over the public address comes, '8 faults, no time faults, total 8'.

I now explain to Jack that he would find in the conditions of a Table A competition the speed might vary. In this case it is fixed at 400 m per minute (437 yds). The course will have been measured by its builder and it's one of 800 m (875 yds), so the rider must complete it within two minutes. If he exceeds the time allowed, he'll be penalized one quarter of a fault for every second or part of a second over the time allowed.

400 m is in fact a fast pace. Indoors it would more likely have been 350 m (383 yds) per minute.

Jack was surprised how quickly each competitor entered; there were no delays. I told him that each had to go on within one minute of getting his call from a steward, or be eliminated. So naturally they were on the alert.

As a second horse jumped a perfect round without fault, Jack enquired if the two would share the prize money.

'Indeed no, the conditions clearly state that if there's a tie for first place, there will be a jump-off. If they're then still equal, time will decide. It also says that those lower in the awards with equal faults will share the appropriate prize money.

'Sometimes under Table A, time will count in the first round to decide the placings; sometimes the riders are required to jump off a second or third round. But rarely, except in a Grand Prix, will you be expected to jump more than three rounds including the first, which means two jumps-off.

'Now there's a nice horse jumping—oh! what a pity, he's stopped at the last part of that treble, 9C. That'll be 3 faults, and if he stops again an additional 6. He *has* stopped again, that makes 9, and this will be his last chance.'

He does stop a third time and the bell goes.

'What does that bell mean?', says Jack, to which I sadly reply, 'Eliminated for three refusals'.

He'll be allowed to jump one fence on the way out for the horse to regain his confidence. That he does, and leaves the ring.

'My goodness', I remark, 'this next horse is going fast but jumping superbly'. Quietly, aside to Jack, 'I think the rider's being run away with!'

At that moment the bell goes and, yes, he'd jumped fence number 8 but had missed out 7. Well that means elimination for taking the wrong course; but had he not actually jumped number 8, circling and going back to 7, he would only have been penalized 3 faults for refusal or correction of course.

The next horse, a bright chestnut, was going well until he baulked

36. Hartwig Steenken on Simona, Men's World Champion, 1974.

at the double, number 6. And, what a mess! Everything knocked over. The bell rings and the clock is stopped, while I tell Jack that he'll be penalized 3 faults for the refusal and 6 seconds added to his final time, to compensate for rebuilding the fence.

The rebuilding's done, the bell rings, the clock is restarted and off he goes. He stops again, this time at the second fence of the double, 6B, knocking everything down once more. The clock is stopped while the arena party gets to work.

'What happens now?', asks Jack.

'Since it's a combination he must go back and when the course is rebuilt he'll have to jump 6A again.'

The next time he's over, but he's been penalized a total of 9 faults —3 for the first refusal and 6 for the second. Also, to his final time would be added 6 penalty seconds for the first knock down, and 8 seconds for knocking down the second fence in a double. Had it been the third fence in a treble he would have collected 10 penalty seconds. The extra seconds for his refusal at the second part of the double were because theoretically it would take him 2 seconds to get back and re-jump the first part.

We are both heartily glad to see him finish without further fault (and he'd had none before the débâcle), dead on the time allowed, two minutes, but since he has 14 penalty seconds these will be added to his time and this will mean 14 seconds over the time allowed. For this he is penalized one quarter of a fault for every second i.e. in this case $3\frac{1}{2}$ time faults.'

'Well now,' says Jack, 'talk about a cricket analysis! But let me try and tell you: 9 faults for the two refusals, plus penalty seconds for twice stopping the clock. 6 seconds the first time, and 8 seconds the next. A quarter of a fault for each of those 14 penalty seconds makes $3\frac{1}{2}$ faults to add to the previous 9. A grand unlucky total of $12\frac{1}{2}$ faults.'

'Well done indeed!' I exclaim with delight. 'You have picked it up quickly.'

I go on to explain that if a rider exceeds the Time Limit, which is double the Time Allowed, he's eliminated; but it rarely happens unless a horse is stubborn and naps.

The next horse goes very well until, almost at the end, he falls after clearing the water jump. This means 8 faults, and of course the loss of time in remounting. The rider quickly is up again but forgets his whip (hardly necessary when the horse had been going so well). He asks one of the arena party for it, and promptly the bell rings.

37. Janou Lefebvre, France, on Rocket at Copenhagen, Ladies World
Champion 1970 and 1974.

I groan slightly and say, 'Eliminated for unauthorized assistance'.

'That's a bit hard. What would have happened if that chap had
given him the whip without being asked?'

'Still the same I'm afraid, but had it been his glasses or something
causing a risk, they would have allowed it.'

'As it happens,' I add, 'It's really just as well for we already have
seven horses without faults—and there are only seven prizes. The
prize money is well spread in show jumping, unlike racing perhaps,
and under international rules the first prize must never exceed a third
of the total. And there will always be some prize for every four taking
part. This helps towards the expense of keeping horses. Though it
doesn't apply in competitions confined to professional riders: there the
first prize may be £2,000 or more, with only a second and third of
much smaller amounts.'

[117]

'In the competition before us now,' I explain, 'there have been thirty starters, therefore eight prizes.'

'But eight horses have already had clear rounds—is there any point in those who hit a fence early on continuing?'

'If it had been early in the week, a rider might like to give his horse a school, but now after several days of jumping he'll certainly want to retire and rest him . . . Listen, they're making an announcement!'

The commentator tells us that any rider with 4 faults will now be retired.

This competition approaches its end, the course builder hurries around raising certain fences, while over the public address we learn that the jump-off course will be fences 1, 2, 3, 6, 8 and 10, the water. It has been shown on the plan of the course, and the riders won't be allowed to come in again and walk it. Other things being equal, the fastest time will decide the winner.

Jack leans back, very satisfied, and says, 'Honestly it's too easy, I could judge it myself.'

'Yes, certainly it is easy to judge, but there are other minor details for which a rider can be eliminated. In fact there are twenty such. Many are certainly technical, but if they occur our excellent commentator will tell us and explain.'

After the jump-off I continue: 'Competitions differ. In some ways our sport is not unlike steeplechasing. You have major competitions with large forbidding fences—they take great jumping, as in the Grand National. Then you have those with smaller obstacles (though not *that* small), with varying height of fence and length of course, where the onus is on the horse's versatility as a jumper. Finally there are the competitions we're just coming to, in which success depends on your horse's obedience and ability to jump, sometimes smaller fences, at a very fast speed. These come under what's called Table B or Table C.

'In fact, I see the next competition, the Tally Ho Stakes, comes under the rules for Table C. But that's not due to start for fifty minutes, so let's go and have something to eat and drink, and we might look at the trade stands.'

When we return it is to find the course builder making his final check. Here the fences are in the main smaller. The jumping would have to be both accurate and fast for this competition is judged on time.

[118]

38. Captain Raimondo d'Inzeo, Italy, on Litargirio, jumping the log wall at Helsinki in 1952: He was the Individual Gold Medallist at the Rome Olympics in 1960.

When the riders come in to walk the course, it is quickly apparent there are more changes of direction than in the previous class. A rider with a very obedient horse will make up time by taking sharper turns and even jumping on the angle. His dominating thought is—where can I gain time?

'How do we score in this?' Jack inquires.

'Faults for knocking down a fence are always in penalty seconds,' I explain. 'In this particular competition, 6 seconds for a knock down, and these naturally are added to the competitor's time. So the shortest time wins.

'Here the course is 600 m (656 yds), with 16 fences. If it were 500 m (547 yds), also with 16 fences, the penalty would be 5 seconds. There's a definite Table under the international rules.'

In comes the first rider, an attractive lady and Jack says, 'Look at the pace she's going, oh what a turn!' But it's too short. Her horse slips and falls. She quickly remounts and is on her way again.

[119]

39. David Broome, G.B., on Mister Softee, the only horse to have won the European Championship three times, once with David Barker and twice with David Broome.

'What does that fall count against her?' he asks with concern.

'There are no penalties for falling or even refusing in this Table, not as in Table A—except for a third refusal which means elimination. Longer time is your penalty. However, if you exceed Time Allowed, every second over counts one penalty. Look at the clock—Time Allowed is 55 seconds, this lady has taken 57 which adds 2 penalties. Score 59 seconds . . .

'Now watch this horse Grey Lad, he's very fast and obedient in his turns. I think he'll win.'

The last fence comes down at that very moment but he is through the finish in 48 seconds. Add 6 penalty seconds, making a final score of 54—and he did ultimately win.

'Yes, even with a knock down,' I point out to Jack later, 'a horse going very fast in these Table C competitions can be the winner.'

Table B I have left until the end for it is seldom used, and then only if the course is less than 700 m (765 yds). Penalties are in seconds, as with Table C, but it is always ten for a knock down.

There are various technical breaches of the rules, in each category, as already mentioned. Among the most serious: failing to start in time, receiving outside assistance, leaving the arena dismounted without permission of the judges, starting before the bell has sounded—all these entail elimination.

On our way home Jack was most enthusiastic. 'Now you have explained everything, not only about the rules but also the background of the organization, I am determined to encourage the Committee of our local show. If only it were run with such smoothness as this there would be many more spectators and competitors. A job well done is always an achievement. Everyone will have the greater pleasure and satisfaction.'